Igniting Change
The BonFire Principles for Transforming Toxic Organizations

DR. CHRISTOPHER BONN
DR. LEANNE SALAZAR-MONTOYA

Igniting Change: The BonFire Principles for Transforming Toxic Organizations

Dr. Christopher Bonn

Dr. LeAnne Salazar-Montoya

Published by BonFire Leadership Solutions LLC

Assisted by www.diverseskillscenter.com

All rights reserved. No part of this book may be reproduced or transmitted in any form or by any means without written permission from the author.

Int. Copyright 2023 © CI-421397657

All rights reserved.

ISBN: 979-8-9882554-3-7
Printed in the U.S.A.

TABLE OF CONTENTS

Dedication: 6
Acknowledgment: 7

Introduction: From Ashes to Excellence: 12
- Overview of the BonFire Principles and their origin
- The importance of addressing toxic organizations
- The transformative power of the BonFire Principles in various sectors

Principle 1: Keep it Vanilla - Simplifying Systems for Success ..31
- The importance of simplicity and clarity in organizational systems
- Case studies demonstrating the effectiveness of simplified systems.
- Strategies for streamlining processes and eliminating unnecessary bureaucracy.

Principle 2: Don't Feed Monsters - Addressing Dysfunctional Dynamics: 43
- Identifying and addressing toxic behaviors and individuals within an organization
- Techniques for preventing the development of destructive patterns.
- Empirical research on the impact of healthy dynamics on organizational success

Principle 3: Water Flowers, Not Weeds - Nurturing Talent and Growth: 59
- Recognizing and fostering potential within an organization
- Strategies for developing a growth mindset and supporting professional development.
- The Role of effective performance management systems in promoting growth

Principle 4: You are PR - Crafting a Positive
Organizational Image 73
- The significance of a strong organizational brand and public image
- Best practices for effective communication and public relations strategies
- Case studies illustrating the impact of a positive image on organizational success.

Principle 5: Stay in Your Lane - Fostering Specialization and
Collaboration: 83
- The importance of specialized roles and clear responsibilities within an organization
- Techniques for promoting collaboration and teamwork.
- Research on the benefits of specialization and collaboration in organizations

Principle 6: Have Fun - Cultivating a Healthy Work Culture: 95
- The significance of a positive work culture in reducing toxicity and promoting success
- Strategies for encouraging work-life balance and fostering a fun environment.
- Empirical evidence on the impact of a healthy work culture on organizational performance

Principle 7: Influence - Leveraging Leadership
for Lasting Change: 109

- The Role of effective leadership in driving organizational transformation
- Techniques for developing influential leaders and cultivating leadership skills.
- Case studies on the impact of strong leadership in transforming toxic organizations.

Conclusion: Sustaining the Flame - Maintaining Success through
the BonFire Principles: 124

- Review of the BonFire Principles and their application in various contexts
- Strategies for ongoing improvement and maintaining long-term success.
- The Future of the BonFire Principles and their potential impact on organizations worldwide

Appendix: Empirical Evidence, Case Studies, and Methodologies: 130

- Detailed analysis of research studies, empirical evidence, and case studies supporting the BonFire Principles
- Overview of the methodologies used in the research and case studies.

Dr. Leanna Salazar-Montoya Bio: 143

Dr. Christopher Bonn Bio: 146

Contact: 148

DEDICATION

This book is lovingly dedicated to Coaches Richard Sanchez, Terry Seward, Don Klostreich, and Raul Nido. It is my humble tribute to the profound lessons you have imparted, the unwavering guidance you have provided, and the formidable challenges you have placed in my path, which have honed me into the person I am today. Your relentless belief in my potential has not only charted the course of my professional journey but has also endowed me with the strength to surmount obstacles and forge innovative solutions.

Each of you has etched an indelible mark on countless young lives, nurturing them into remarkable parents, compassionate family members, influential leaders, and responsible citizens. The ripples of your impact have flowed far and wide, effecting change in the world and transforming the lives of multitudes.

Above all, I dedicate this book to my Lord and Savior, Jesus Christ. Through His abundant grace and divine guidance, I have found the strength to surmount trials and the wisdom to navigate life's complexities. His words in Philippians 4:13, "I can do all this through him who gives me strength," have been a beacon of light in the dark, a source of solace during trials, and a reminder of His everlasting presence in my life.

To my esteemed mentors and my Savior, I dedicate this work to you with profound gratitude and reverence. Thank you for being the guiding stars of my journey.

ACKNOWLEDGMENT

To all the indomitable leaders who have breathed life into their organizations, turning them from ashes to radiant flames of success, this acknowledgment is for you.

To you, who have braved the inferno of chaos and toxicity, who have taken failing organizations in your hands, shaping, and molding them into beacons of success and excellence. You, who has stared down the daunting precipice of organizational collapse and dared to initiate the difficult journey towards transformation with steadfast resolve and unyielding determination.

Your sacrifice and commitment are beyond commendable. You have poured your heart and soul into your endeavors, often at the expense of your personal lives, health, and peace of mind. You have willingly placed yourselves in the line of fire, weathering the hailstorm of politics, societal expectations, and community scrutiny.

Behind every thriving organization is a leader like you—courageous, innovative, and inspiring. Your tenacity serves as a beacon, lighting the path for others to follow. Your courage stirs up the spirit of endurance in those around you. Your unyielding desire for excellence fuels the fires of ambition, sparking transformation in the hearts of your teams and within your organizations.

To those who stepped onto the battlefield with the noblest of intentions only to be besieged by insurmountable challenges and barriers, I see you. Your intentions were pure, your steps courageous. While you may have been crushed under the weight of the colossal task, your effort was not in vain. Your journey is not defined by the fall but by your willingness to rise again.

Know that your attempt, bravery, and initiative are recognized and celebrated. Cherish your small victories, for they are steppingstones to grand success. Keep pushing, keep striving, and remember, success lies just beyond the horizon for those who refuse to give up.

In acknowledgment of your spirit, your sacrifice, and your unwavering resolve, I salute you. I celebrate you. May you inspire, transform, and lead with courage, passion, and steadfast resilience. This acknowledgment is my salute to your enduring spirit and unyielding resolve. Keep the flame alive.

In the ever-evolving landscape of education, the role of school leaders has never been more critical. As we embark on a journey to explore leadership concepts and ideas for school leaders, we are venturing into a realm that not only shapes the future of individual students but also the future of our society as a whole. This forward serves as a prelude to a profound exploration of leadership in the context of schools—a vital and complex arena where vision, dedication, and innovation converge.

This book is a collection of thoughts, ideas, and best practices from a pair of practitioners who have positioned themselves to use their lived experiences to leverage their knowledge, successes, and failures to help a new generation of leaders. While no one person, group, or organization has all the answers, what we offer is honest, practical, and doable actions to move your institution forward.

Dr. Christopher Bonn has spent his career working in some of the most challenging districts in the American Southwest and serving children in underserved communities. He, along with me, Dr. LeAnne Salazar Montoya, has dedicated our lives to advocacy, turning around schools, and giving voice to the often voiceless. Collectively, we offer a wealth of knowledge, expertise, and knowledge from the school of hard knocks. When you are an advocate for those most in need, it can at times be an uphill battle, and more times than not, a lonely but worthwhile journey to provide resources for our most precious treasures, the future, our children!!

While leadership comes with its expected challenges, change can sometimes be an unpopular decision but a necessary one! They say we can't keep doing what we have always done because we will always get what we always got, and that isn't always what we need! Change can often-times be met with some resistance, but the benefits we reap come with time. Leadership comes many times after making mistakes, humbling ourselves, and then learning from the mistakes to make more informed decisions later!

The essence of leadership in education extends far beyond the confines of traditional notions of authority. It transcends mere management and administration to encompass a dynamic and multifaceted role that influences the lives of students, teachers, parents, and the community at large. To be a school leader is to be a steward of both educational excellence and social progress.

In the pages that follow, we will embark on a journey to dissect the art and science of leadership in the realm of education. We will delve into the core principles and ideas that underpin effective school leadership, drawing from a rich tapestry of theories, experiences, and best practices. Whether you are an experienced school leader seeking fresh insights or a novice aspiring to lead with purpose and impact, this book offers a treasure trove of wisdom and guidance.

We will explore topics ranging from visionary leadership and emotional intelligence to fostering a culture of innovation and building strong relationships within a school community. Throughout, we will emphasize the importance of ethical leadership, equity, and inclusivity, for these principles are the bedrock upon which exemplary schools are built.

As we traverse the landscape of educational leadership, we will encounter stories of real-life leaders who have navigated the challenges and triumphs of their roles. Their experiences will serve as beacons of inspiration, illuminating the path for those who follow in their footsteps.

Above all, this book is a testament to the enduring power of leadership to transform lives and shape the future. It is a call to action, an invitation to engage in a lifelong journey of self-improvement, collaboration, and unwavering commitment to the betterment of education.

So, as we embark on this voyage into the heart of educational leadership, let us be mindful of the immense responsibility that rests on the shoulders of school leaders. Let us be open to the wisdom of the past and the innovations of the present as we carve out a brighter future for our students and our world.
May this exploration of leadership concepts and ideas be a source of inspiration, enlightenment, and empowerment

for school leaders, present and future, who hold the key to shaping the next generation and, by extension, the destiny of humankind. Let the journey begin!

INTRODUCTION
FROM ASHES TO EXCELLENCE

The BonFire Principles and Their Origin

The BonFire Principles were born from a series of invaluable experiences and lessons learned throughout my career, beginning in 1991 when I started working in schools. My journey began at my alma mater, where the high school principal recruited me to join the varsity football coaching staff. At the time, the once-dominant football program struggled, with 22 consecutive losses. However, the arrival of a new head coach, who had previously led a nationally recognized wrestling dynasty, marked a turning point for the team.

This new head coach quickly surrounded himself with the most talented coaching staff in the state, and I was honored to be invited to join straight out of college. Working alongside these exceptional individuals, I was exposed to a wealth of knowledge and experience that would later inform the BonFire Principles. These principles, although not yet branded as such, guided my leadership and decision-making throughout my career.

It was not until I became the principal of a failing high school that I was forced to reflect on these early lessons and adapt my behaviors to drive positive change and keep my job. I recognized the power of the first principle, inspired by the head football coach's approach to hiring the best talent and granting them the autonomy to do their jobs. He stayed in his lane, refrained from interfering or micromanaging, and allowed his staff to flourish.

Over time, I began synthesizing and refining these lessons into coherent principles, which I later branded the BonFire Principles. These principles have since been applied to various organizations in different sectors, enabling them to rise from the ashes of failure and achieve excellence. The BonFire Principles are as follows:

1. Keep it Vanilla: Simplify systems and processes for maximum efficiency and effectiveness.

2. Don't Feed Monsters: Identify and address toxic behaviors and individuals within an organization.

3. Water Flowers, Not Weeds: Nurture talent and foster growth among your team members.

4. You are PR: Cultivate a positive organizational image and strong brand identity.

5. Stay in Your Lane: Encourage specialization and collaboration, allowing each individual to excel in their expertise.

6. Have Fun: Create a healthy work culture that supports work-life balance and employee satisfaction.

7. Influence: Embrace strong leadership to drive lasting change and inspire others to follow suit.

These BonFire Principles offer a roadmap for transforming toxic organizations into thriving, successful entities. By understanding their origins and the experiences that shaped them, we can better appreciate the power of these principles to ignite change and propel organizations to new heights of excellence.

In each toxic organization I encountered, I recognized the parallels to the failing football program I had helped rescue at the start of my career. These organizations were plagued with a myriad of issues: mismanagement of fiscal resources leading to extreme budget deficits; a lack of quality and effective staff, either due to constant turnover or the hiring of non-qualified and inefficient employees; and a decline in reputation as top-performing students left for better schools, further impacting the budget and overall academic achievement.

Student and staff attendance suffered as motivation waned, burdening the organization's financial stability. Time and again, leaders were brought in to turn these organizations around, but they were unsuccessful. My younger, more egotistical self-believed I could outwork the challenges and demand excellence. However, as Mike Tyson once said, "We all have a game plan until we get punched." I was punched, and I realized that my initial approach was flawed.

Faced with the harsh reality of the challenges before me, I understood that I needed to find practical solutions and strategies that would yield immediate results, or I would fail just like those who came before me. This realization led me to revisit and refine the BonFire Principles, which had served me well in the earlier stages of my career. These principles became the foundation for my approach to rescuing these toxic organizations.

By applying the BonFire Principles systematically and thoughtfully, I was able to quickly rebrand the organizations, exponentially improving their performance and results. I addressed the staffing issues by recruiting and retaining quality and adequate staff, fostering an environment where they could thrive and grow. I also implemented sustainable systems that helped rescue the organizations from fiscal turmoil.

In each case, the BonFire Principles proved to be a powerful tool for transforming these struggling organizations into successful, high-performing entities. By sharing these principles and the experiences that shaped them, I hope other leaders and organizations can learn from my journey and apply these principles to their unique situations, ultimately achieving the same level of success and excellence I have witnessed firsthand.

Much like the 0-22 football program, where athletes had lost pride and motivation to attend practice, I faced similar challenges in my first leadership roles within toxic organizations. Students and staff were disengaged and demotivated, seeking more exciting and attractive alternatives, which were only sometimes the safest or most legal options. Recruiting talented individuals and motivating them to commit to the organization's goals proved daunting.

Reflecting on the genius of the head coach who turned around the failing football program, I recalled his strategic approach to gain the most influence. He recognized that improving performance required athletes to be bigger, faster, and more robust, making strength, agility, and conditioning paramount. Rather than simply demanding attendance, he developed a Public Relations campaign, raised funds to upgrade the weight room facilities, purchased new equipment, and created a recognizable brand and slogan.

Offering enticing incentives, such as branded clothing items, the head coach fostered a sense of pride, belonging, and connection among the athletes, encouraging their participation in strength, agility, and conditioning programs. His strategy proved successful, with the number of student-athletes increasing from around 32 to approximately 175, necessitating expanded facilities to accommodate the growth.

This experience taught me two vital principles: "You are PR" and "Influence." I soon adopted and branded these concepts as part of the BonFire Principles. In my subsequent leadership roles, I utilized these principles to address the challenges faced by toxic organizations. By focusing on creating a positive image, fostering a sense of pride, and belonging, and strategically managing the areas with tremendous potential for influence, I motivated and engaged the members of these organizations.

Drawing from these lessons and experiences, I crafted the BonFire Principles to provide a roadmap for other leaders facing similar challenges. By applying these principles, leaders can transform struggling organizations into thriving, high-performing entities. The principles of "You are PR" and "Influence" are essential to this transformation, inspiring pride, commitment, and positive change.

The BonFire Principles, forged from my early experiences in coaching and leadership roles, provide a robust framework for transforming struggling organizations into thriving, high-performing entities. These principles, which include "You are PR" and "Influence," are vital components of organizational change, fostering pride, commitment, and a positive environment.

The principle "You are PR" emphasizes the importance of creating a positive image for an organization, both internally and externally. A solid public relations campaign can help change the perception of a struggling organization, making it more appealing to talented individuals and stakeholders. In the case of the 0-22 football program, upgrading the weight room facilities, purchasing new equipment, and developing a recognizable brand and slogan were essential in creating a sense of pride and belonging among the athletes.

To effectively apply the "You are PR" principle within a struggling organization, leaders should focus on several key aspects:

1. Develop a strong brand identity: A well-defined brand identity can create a sense of unity and belonging among members of the organization. This can be achieved using logos, slogans, and visual elements representing the organization's values and goals.

2. Invest in resources: Providing necessary resources, such as upgraded facilities and equipment, can demonstrate a commitment to the organization's success and improve the overall environment for its members.

3. Communicate effectively: Open, transparent communication can help build trust and confidence in the organization's leadership, fostering a more positive culture.

The principle of "Influence" highlights the importance of identifying and addressing the areas with the most significant potential for impact to create lasting, positive change. In the case of the football program, the head coach recognized that solid and athletic players are necessary for the team to succeed. By focusing on strength, agility, and conditioning, he influenced the athletes to participate and improve, ultimately leading to the program's turnaround.

To apply the "Influence" principle effectively, leaders should:

1. Identify critical areas of concern: Analyze the organization's current challenges and determine which areas, if addressed, could lead to the most remarkable improvements.

2. Develop targeted strategies: Create specific, measurable plans to address the identified areas of concern, focusing on achievable goals and clear milestones.

3. Monitor progress: Regularly assess the organization's progress in addressing key areas of concern, adjusting strategies to ensure continued improvement.

4. Celebrate successes: Recognize and celebrate the organization's and its members' achievements, reinforcing a sense of pride and commitment to the overall goals.

Integrating the principles of "You are PR" and "Influence" into their leadership approach, leaders can transform struggling organizations into thriving, high-performing entities. The BonFire Principles provide a roadmap for navigating the challenges of organizational change, inspiring pride, commitment, and positive growth for all involved.

The head coach understood that the path to success would demand hard work and dedication from everyone involved in the team. He recognized the importance of incorporating fun with athletes and coaches facing grueling workouts in extreme conditions, long workdays, and additional commitments. He knew that to maintain motivation and dedication, it was essential to make the environment enjoyable.

The coach created a fun atmosphere by playing loud music preferred by the students, incorporating entertaining, competitive activities that also developed athletic skills, and scheduling practices and events in popular vacation destinations. He understood that if the athletes and coaches enjoyed themselves, their hard work would feel less like a chore and more like play. This approach resulted in a team that was committed and eager to excel.

I realized the same principle could be applied to the schools and organizations I led. While we often focused on making the environment enjoyable for the students, paying attention to the staff's well-being was crucial. The staff's mood heavily influences the overall atmosphere within an organization, and a happy team leads to happy students. Creating a fun, welcoming, and exciting environment is vital for everyone's success.

The key takeaways from this experience can be summarized as follows:

1. Integrate fun and excitement: Incorporate enjoyable activities into the routine that contribute to skill development and growth. This can foster motivation and commitment among team members.

2. Focus on everyone's well-being: Ensuring a fun and welcoming atmosphere for staff and students is essential, as their happiness and satisfaction directly impact the organization's success.

3. Balance work and play: Recognize that hard work and dedication can be more sustainable if combined with elements of fun and enjoyment. This can lead to a more engaged and enthusiastic team.

4. Set a positive tone: A happy and enthusiastic leadership team can inspire similar attitudes among staff and students, creating a more productive and positive environment.

Applying these lessons to transforming toxic or struggling organizations, leaders can create an environment where everyone feels engaged and motivated, from staff to students. Fun, enjoyment, and enthusiasm can become powerful tools in turning around a failing organization and fostering success for all involved.

Continuing with the theme of fostering a fun, welcoming, and exciting environment, it is crucial to understand how this approach can impact various aspects of a struggling organization. By integrating fun and excitement into the daily routine, leaders can create a more vibrant and dynamic atmosphere that translates into tangible improvements in staff morale, student engagement, and overall organizational performance.

To further enhance the relevance of this section, consider the following strategies:

1. Celebrate successes, big and small: Acknowledge and appreciate staff and students' accomplishments, promoting a culture of recognition and boosting morale. Regular celebrations and rewards can help maintain motivation and dedication, even during challenging times.

2. Encourage creativity and innovation: Provide opportunities for staff and students to express their ideas and collaborate on innovative projects or initiatives. This can foster a sense of ownership and pride in their work while adding fun and excitement to their daily activities.

3. Organize team-building activities: Arrange regular team-building events that allow staff and students to bond and develop strong relationships. These activities can promote camaraderie, enhance communication, and provide a more supportive and enjoyable work environment.

4. Prioritize work-life balance: Encourage staff to balance their professional and personal lives, promoting self-care and overall well-being. A healthy work-life balance can lead to happier staff, reduced burnout, and improved performance.

5. Create opportunities for professional development: Offer training and development programs that enable staff to grow professionally and personally. Providing opportunities for

learning and growth can make the workplace more engaging and enjoyable.

6. Foster a culture of open communication: Encourage staff and students to share their thoughts, concerns, and ideas openly and honestly. This can help build trust and create a more inclusive and supportive environment where everyone feels valued and heard.

By incorporating these strategies, leaders can further enhance the relevance of their approach to transforming struggling organizations. A fun, welcoming, and exciting environment contributes to the happiness and satisfaction of staff and students and significantly impacts the organization's overall success and performance. By prioritizing the well-being and enjoyment of all members, leaders can create a thriving and sustainable organization that achieves lasting success.

In my early days as a wrestler under the guidance of the new football coach, who was also the head of the wrestling dynasty, I recall being frustrated by the relentless focus on practicing take-downs. We spent 90%, if not the entire practice, on this aspect of wrestling, with very little time on mat work. The coach believed that if we excelled in taking our opponents down, we would rarely have to worry about escaping or defending against takedowns. As a young athlete, I couldn't grasp the simplicity of this approach, thinking that being part of a national wrestling dynasty would involve more complexity.

This same concept of simplicity and unwavering focus was applied when the coach transitioned to leading the football team. He decided that our group would have at most eight core plays, which would serve as the foundation of our strategy. He would always revert to these core principles in challenging situations or when the game was close rather than introducing trick plays or adding complexity. Over time, we expanded our offensive and defensive strategies, but only once we had mastered the foundational concepts.

This "keep it vanilla" approach has guided my efforts to transform struggling organizations. Often, these organizations have elaborate strategic plans with dozens of goals and countless moving parts. Despite the effort invested in creating these plans, they are rarely implemented with fidelity. Most administrators, governing board members, and staff cannot summarize these complex plans effectively. What's more, the implemented portions are done with mediocrity.

The issue is the need for simplicity and a laser-like focus on doing a few things exceptionally well before adding more layers of complexity. Successful organizations have a niche and excel in that area, often to the point of perfection. By embracing this "keep it vanilla" philosophy and prioritizing mastery of core principles, organizations can lay the foundation for sustainable success and long-term improvement. This introduction will emphasize the importance of simplicity, clarity, and unwavering focus on the essentials, demonstrating how these principles can transform struggling organizations into thriving, high-performing entities.

The "Keep it Vanilla" concept emphasizes the importance of simplicity and focus in driving organizational success. Often, leaders and organizations claim to adhere to principles such as KISS (keep it simple, stupid), laser-like focus, and the 80-20 rule, but their actions and strategies belie these claims. Instead of keeping things straightforward, they complicate their efforts, making it nearly impossible to implement their plans or achieve their goals effectively.

The "Keep it Vanilla" principle reminds leaders that the key to rescuing struggling organizations is to identify critical, influential strategies, behaviors, or techniques and to become obsessively dedicated to their execution. Just as someone who can only eat vanilla would not entertain the thought of trying chocolate, great organizations must be unwavering in their focus on a few select strategies and resist the temptation to stray from their core mission.

In practice, this means identifying the essential elements that will lead to improvement and growth and concentrating all efforts on perfecting these elements. This could be a specific teaching method in an educational setting, a unique product offering in a business, or a streamlined process that sets the organization apart from others. By keeping it vanilla, organizations can avoid burnout and confusion from juggling too many tasks or initiatives simultaneously.

To truly embrace the "Keep it Vanilla" principle, leaders must ensure that their organizations commit to this simplicity and focus. They must relentlessly pursue excellence in crucial areas, building on and enhancing their strengths. By doing so, they can foster a culture of mastery and continuous improvement, ultimately transforming their struggling organizations into thriving, successful ones.

As we delve into the final principles of transforming struggling organizations, it is crucial to understand the role of negativity and how to combat it effectively. Individuals thrive on criticism, attacking others, and undermining progress in every organization. These "monsters" are seemingly insatiable, growing more extensive and destructive the more attention they receive. The best way to neutralize their impact is to stop feeding them, to starve them of the attention they so desperately crave.

Great leaders recognize the futility of trying to appease these monsters or satisfy their endless demands. Instead, they focus on nurturing positivity, embracing the concept of "Watering Flowers, Not Weeds." By choosing to celebrate the small successes, praising the efforts of their organization and team, and promoting a culture of encouragement and support, these leaders create an environment where negativity struggles to gain a foothold.

However, starving monsters is a challenging task. As their influence wanes, they become more aggressive, targeting the leader, their family, teammates, and friends. When these tactics fail, they may resort to character assassination, aiming to undermine the organization, team, and leadership by any means necessary. Their goal is not always to see the organization fail but to assert control, gain attention, or sow fear.

Monsters are typically individuals who lack self-confidence and have a negative self-image. They feel compelled to attack and belittle others to bolster their perceived worth, intelligence, or importance. To effectively counteract their impact, leaders must remain steadfast in their commitment to "Don't Feed Monsters and Water Flowers, Not Weeds."

Adopting this principle, leaders can create a more compelling and positive atmosphere for their organization, fostering a culture where progress, growth, and collaboration can thrive. By starving monsters of the attention, they crave and nurturing the positive elements within the organization, leaders can empower their teams and set the stage for lasting, transformative success.

The key to transforming struggling, failing, or toxic organizations lies in embracing simple, yet powerful concepts learned not from academic textbooks but from real-life experiences in coaching athletics. When faced with difficult situations, reflecting on these principles can provide effective, non-traditional solutions that lead to lasting success.

First, successful leaders identify the critical factors that significantly influence improvement and focus on these areas with a laser-like intensity. By fostering a sense of pride, belonging, and connection through branding and public relations, they can motivate team members to participate and excel.

Next, making organizations fun, welcoming, and exciting cannot be overstated. By creating an enjoyable atmosphere where everyone is engaged, leaders can boost the morale and performance of staff and students, leading to happier and more successful organizations.
The "keeping it vanilla" principle emphasizes the need for a focused approach. By mastering foundational concepts and building upon

them, organizations can achieve excellence in their niche, ensuring that all efforts are directed toward meaningful progress.

Finally, leaders must confront negativity head-on, refusing to feed the "monsters" that thrive on criticism and conflict. By watering the flowers and not the weeds, they can foster a culture of positivity, encouragement, and support, enabling their organization to grow and flourish.

By applying these simple yet profound principles, leaders can effectively transform struggling organizations, drawing on the wisdom gained from real-life experiences in athletics to create lasting change and success.

Section: Addressing Toxic Organizations - The Importance and Implications

Toxic organizations pose a significant threat not only to the success and growth of the organization itself but also to the well-being of its members. Understanding the importance of addressing toxic organizations is vital for leaders and administrators who strive to foster a healthy and productive working environment. In this section, we delve into the implications of toxic organizations, the consequences of inaction, and the necessity of intervention for long-term success.

Impact on Employee Well-being and Retention

A pervasive culture of negativity, hostility, and unhealthy competition characterizes toxic organizations. This environment can severely affect employees' mental and emotional well-being, increasing stress, burnout, and dissatisfaction. When faced with a toxic work environment, talented and dedicated employees are likelier to seek employment elsewhere, resulting in a high turnover rate and a loss of valuable human resources.

A decline in Productivity and Performance

A toxic organizational culture can create a significant barrier to productivity and performance. Employees working in such an environment often need help with motivation, focus, and engagement. The constant stress and negativity can hinder creativity and problem-solving skills, ultimately leading to a decline in overall performance. This decline can cascade, further exacerbating the toxic culture and stifling growth.

Damage to Reputation and Brand

The reputation of an organization is one of its most valuable assets. Toxic organizations can suffer severe damage to their reputation and brand, both internally and externally. Word of mouth and negative reviews can spread quickly, impacting the organization's ability to attract top talent, clients, or customers. A tarnished reputation can take years to rebuild and, in some cases, may never fully recover.

Legal and Financial Implications

Toxic organizations may face legal and financial consequences due to their unhealthy work environment. Lawsuits for harassment, discrimination, or workplace safety can result in costly settlements and damage the organization's reputation. Moreover, the financial implications of high employee turnover and low productivity can strain an organization's resources.

The Necessity of Intervention

Given the severe consequences of toxic organizations, leaders must intervene and address these issues proactively. By recognizing the signs of toxicity, leaders can take steps to confront the problem and implement strategies for positive change. Failure to act can perpetuate a toxic culture, putting the entire organization at risk.

Addressing toxic organizations is paramount for long-term success and sustainability. By understanding the implications of a toxic work environment, leaders can take decisive action to transform the culture, support employee well-being, and promote a more positive and productive atmosphere. This book's simple yet profound principles provide a valuable framework for tackling the complex challenge of transforming toxic organizations and fostering a culture of success and growth.

A Real-Life Sporting Team Example - The Transformation of the Golden State Warriors

The Golden State Warriors, a professional basketball team in the NBA, provide a compelling real-life example of how addressing toxicity within an organization can lead to remarkable success. In the early 2010s, the Warriors faced numerous challenges, including internal conflicts, poor performance, and a negative organizational culture. However, strategic changes and a focus on fostering a positive environment made the team one of the most successful franchises in recent NBA history (Kaufman, 2015).

The Warriors' transformation began with the arrival of new ownership, Joe Lacob and Peter Guber, in 2010. Recognizing the need for a cultural shift, the new owners made several key decisions, including hiring Bob Myers as general manager and Steve Kerr as head coach. These leaders prioritized creating a positive, inclusive, supportive team culture, emphasizing communication, collaboration, and trust among players and staff (Kaufman, 2015).

One of the most significant changes made under Kerr's leadership was the focus on player development and a strong emphasis on teamwork. By implementing an offensive system that prioritized ball movement and unselfish play, the Warriors were able to unlock the full potential of their roster, including stars Stephen Curry, Klay Thompson, and Draymond Green (Medina, 2018).

As a result of these strategic changes and the fostering of a positive organizational culture, the Warriors experienced unprecedented success, winning NBA championships in 2015, 2017, and 2018. The transformation of the Golden State Warriors is an inspiring example of how addressing toxicity and implementing a solid organizational culture can lead to remarkable success in the world of sports.

A Real-Life Fortune 500 Company Example - The Transformation of Microsoft

Microsoft, one of the world's most valuable Fortune 500 companies, offers a real-life example of how addressing organizational challenges and fostering a positive culture can lead to significant success. After experiencing stagnation and internal conflicts in the early 2010s, Microsoft underwent a dramatic transformation under CEO Satya Nadella, who took the helm in 2014 (Ovide, 2018).

One of Nadella's priorities was shifting the company's culture from highly competitive and siloed to emphasizing collaboration, learning, and innovation. He introduced the concept of a "growth mindset" to the organization, encouraging employees to embrace challenges, learn from failure, and continuously improve (Copeland, 2018).

In addition to cultural changes, Nadella made strategic decisions that propelled Microsoft into new markets and technologies. He focused on cloud computing, artificial intelligence, and other emerging areas, resulting in the rapid growth of Microsoft's Azure cloud platform and the successful launch of products like HoloLens and Surface devices (Ovide, 2018).

Under Nadella's leadership, Microsoft experienced a remarkable turnaround, with its stock price more than tripling between 2014 and 2018 and the company regaining its position as one of the world's most valuable tech firms (Lashinsky, 2018). Microsoft's transformation is a powerful example of how addressing organizational challenges and fostering a positive culture can lead to significant success in the corporate world.

The Universality of the Principles for Success

The principles we have explored thus far, drawn from sports coaching and organizational leadership, apply to all domains. These principles are remarkably versatile and can be adapted to various contexts, including enterprises, teams, sports, organizations, schools, and personal life.

First, identifying critical areas of influence and focusing on them to bring about significant improvements is a lesson that can be applied across various settings. Regardless of the context, it is crucial to determine the most critical factors that can drive change and devote resources to them rather than diluting efforts across numerous initiatives. This targeted approach can lead to more impactful results, whether in a corporate boardroom, a sports team's locker room, or personal goal setting.

Second, fostering a fun, welcoming, and engaging environment is universally relevant. People thrive in atmospheres where they feel motivated, supported, and connected to others. This principle can be applied in diverse contexts, such as creating an inclusive corporate culture, making a classroom more engaging for students, or nurturing a supportive family environment at home.

Third, the concept of "*keeping it vanilla*" underscores the importance of mastering foundational skills and strategies before expanding into more complex areas. This approach can benefit various settings, from a company refining its core products or services to an athlete honing their fundamental techniques. By focusing on what truly matters and perfecting those aspects, individuals and organizations can set themselves up for long-term success.

Finally, the principles of "*Don't Feed Monsters*" and "*Water Flowers, Not Weeds*" remind us to focus on the positive aspects and not to get derailed by negativity. This mindset can be transformative in any context, as it encourages individuals and organizations to celebrate successes, foster positive relationships, and remain resilient in the face of challenges.

In conclusion, the principles discussed in this introductory chapter are not confined to any specific domain. They are universal lessons that can be applied interchangeably in enterprises, the military, teams, sports, organizations, schools, and personal life. They offer invaluable guidance for anyone seeking to foster positive change and lasting success.

I branded the BonFire Principles as my leadership principles, and I have spent the last 17 years researching and trying to understand their empirical significance. The proof is in the results. Working in large urban settings and small rural communities in Arizona, California, and New Mexico, these concepts have been shared throughout the United States through leadership mentoring, coaching, and consultation. They have been used successfully in athletics and large organizations alike. The system is robust and dynamic enough to meet the needs of any organization and leader. The key is staying authentic and disciplined.

Many experts will argue that change takes 3-5 years. Unfortunately, in many situations, you don't have 3-5 years to change; the organization will cease, or you will be unemployed. Not to mention the countless children, clients, customers, and spectators that could be affected or perish as a result. Change can happen overnight. It takes 3-5 years to make these changes consistent and sustainable.

With the BonFire Principles, you can see exponential results quickly. If you maintain discipline and fidelity, you can build sustainable systems that are effective, efficient, and successful. These principles offer a robust framework for transforming struggling, failing, or toxic organizations, and they have the potential to create lasting, positive change in a variety of settings.

The results you observe in any organization directly reflect how the system is designed to perform. If you desire better outcomes, blaming people, complaining, criticizing, or making excuses is not productive. Instead, focus on changing the system to achieve the desired performance. By addressing the underlying structure and processes, you can create a more effective and efficient system that leads to success and drives your desired results.

Principle 1:
Keep it Vanilla - Simplifying Systems for Success

In today's fast-paced and complex world, organizations face an ever-increasing number of challenges that demand efficient and effective solutions (Kotter, 1996; Senge, 1990). Navigating these challenges requires leadership adept at simplifying systems and processes to foster success (Covey, 1989; Fullan, 2001; Bonn, 2023). Principle 1: Keep it Vanilla - Simplifying Systems for Success explores the importance of clarity and simplicity in organizational systems, offering leaders practical guidance on streamlining processes and eliminating unnecessary bureaucracy.

The chapter begins by examining the significance of simplicity and clarity in organizational systems (Bonn, 2023; Covey, 1989). Drawing from the collective wisdom of our esteemed authors and researchers, this section highlights the benefits of simplification, including improved communication (Fullan, 2001), increased productivity (Kotter, 1996), and enhanced decision-making (Senge, 1990).

Following this foundational exploration, the chapter delves into real-world case studies demonstrating simplified systems' effectiveness (Kotter, 1996; Senge, 1990; Fullan, 2001). These examples showcase organizations that have successfully transformed their operations by embracing the "Keep it Vanilla" principle, leading to increased efficiency and overall success (Bonn, 2023).

Finally, the chapter provides practical strategies for streamlining processes and cutting through bureaucratic red tape (Covey, 1989; Kotter, 1996; Fullan, 2001; Senge, 1990; Bonn, 2023). Leaders will learn how to implement these tactics in their organizations, promoting a culture of simplicity that empowers individuals at every level to thrive.

Together, these sections offer a comprehensive guide to embracing simplicity in organizational systems, providing leaders with the tools they need to navigate today's complex landscape confidently and easily (Kotter, 1996; Senge, 1990; Covey, 1989; Fullan, 2001; Bonn, 2023). Organizations can unlock their full potential and achieve lasting success in an ever-changing world by keeping it vanilla.

Organizations can unlock their full potential and achieve lasting success in an ever-changing world by keeping it vanilla. In today's rapidly changing and complex environment, organizations face many challenges requiring efficient and effective solutions (Kotter, 1996; Senge, 1990). This is particularly evident in education, where leaders must address many pressing issues. These issues include teaching social-emotional skills (Durlak, Weissberg, Dymnicki, Taylor, & Schellinger, 2011), counseling students (Erford, 2018), feeding hungry children, dealing with school violence and mass shootings (Dorn & Dorn, 2014), managing addiction, child neglect and abandonment, extreme poverty (Fullan, 2010), multilingual learners (Echevarria, Vogt, & Short, 2016), political turmoil (Druker, 2008), declining budgets (Covey, 1989), and competition from private and charter schools. Additionally, leaders must address students' and staff's various identities and needs.

Keeping things simple and straightforward in organizational systems is essential, considering these numerous conflicts and complexities. This chapter, "Principle 1: Keep it Vanilla - Simplifying Systems for Success," will explore the importance of simplicity and clarity in organizational systems. We will discuss case studies demonstrating the effectiveness of simplified systems in various organizations and provide strategies for streamlining processes and eliminating unnecessary bureaucracy. By embracing the "Keep it Vanilla" principle, educational leaders can better navigate their challenges and create an environment that fosters success for all stakeholders.

The Importance of Simplicity and Clarity in Organizational Systems

In an era marked by increasing complexity and competing priorities, the importance of simplicity and clarity in organizational systems cannot be overstated. Organizations that effectively streamline their processes and communicate their objectives can achieve better results, increase employee engagement, and more efficiently allocate resources (Kotter, 1996). This section will examine the benefits of simplicity and clarity in organizational systems and the potential pitfalls of overly complex systems.

One of the most significant benefits of simplicity and clarity in organizational systems is improved decision-making (Covey, 1989). When organizations have clear objectives and straightforward processes, employees are better equipped to make informed decisions that align with the organization's goals (Fullan, 2010). Additionally, a clear and simple organizational structure can help reduce decision fatigue and cognitive overload, which are known to negatively impact performance (Sweller, 1988).

Simplicity and clarity in organizational systems also lead to increased employee engagement and satisfaction (Senge, 1990). When employees understand their roles and responsibilities and how their work contributes to the organization's overall success, they are more likely to be engaged and motivated. In contrast, overly complex systems can create confusion and frustration, leading to disengagement and turnover (Kotter, 1996).

Efficient resource allocation is another benefit of simplicity and clarity in organizational systems (Druker, 2008). When organizations have streamlined processes and clear objectives, they can more effectively allocate human and financial resources to areas that will have the most significant impact (Fullan, 2010). This efficiency can result in significant cost savings and increased productivity.

However, despite the numerous benefits of simplicity and clarity in organizational systems, some organizations need help with overly complex systems. These systems can result from various factors, such as a need for clearer vision, competing priorities, or bureaucratic red tape (Kotter, 1996). When organizations become mired in complexity, they risk decreased efficiency, employee disengagement, and failure to achieve their objectives (Senge, 1990).

Simplicity and clarity in organizational systems are essential for optimal performance, employee engagement, and efficient resource allocation. By focusing on these principles, organizations can better navigate their complex challenges and create an environment that fosters success for all stakeholders.

Adding to the discussion on simplicity and clarity in organizational systems, addressing the pitfalls of well-intentioned leaders who inadvertently add layers of complexity to their organizations is crucial. These leaders often introduce new tasks, programs, and ideas to simplify processes for their staff but fail to remove any existing burdens. This approach increases employee pressure and complicates the organizational structure.

Another common mistake leaders must be aware of is a reluctance to address incompetent, insubordinate, or incapable employees. Instead of tackling the issue head-on through training, development, or, if necessary, termination, they resort to adding more layers of complexity to the system in the form of checks and balances for accountability (Kotter, 1996). This approach paralyzes the organization and demoralizes competent, efficient, and effective employees.

To avoid these pitfalls, influential leaders must possess the courage to confront issues directly, providing support and development opportunities for employees who struggle to meet expectations. If the situation does not improve, they must be willing to make tough decisions, including terminating underperforming employees and hiring suitable replacements (Covey, 1989). Additionally, leaders must be willing to address conflict and make difficult choices to maintain simplicity and clarity in their organizational systems (Senge, 1990).

Organizational leaders must recognize the importance of simplicity and clarity in their systems and avoid the common traps of adding unnecessary layers of complexity. By addressing employee performance issues directly and making tough decisions when needed, leaders can foster an environment that promotes efficiency, effectiveness, and employee satisfaction.

In addition to the factors already discussed, external forces such as political pressure, media scrutiny, misinformation, legislative changes, community climate, and vendor influence can contribute to the complexity of organizational systems (Fullan, 2001). Leaders must be aware of these pressures and understand their potential impact on the organization without allowing them to create unnecessary layers of complexity.

When faced with external pressures, leaders should be prepared to shoulder some of the burdens or, at the very least, work collectively and collaboratively to determine how to integrate new initiatives, protocols, legislations, programs, and procedures without adding layers of complexity (Kotter, 1996). This may involve replacing existing processes rather than simply layering new ones on top of them (Covey, 1989).

Organizations often need to invest more time and resources into implementing new ideas, systems, protocols, procedures, and curricula, which can make them resistant or resistant to change (Fullan, 2001). In these cases, leaders must anticipate potential resistance, prepare their staff, and communicate the need to eliminate, replace, and, most importantly, simplify processes to protect employees and maintain organizational effectiveness and efficiency (Bonn, 2023; Senge, 1990).

By addressing external pressures proactively and making informed decisions about which initiatives to adopt, leaders can prevent the introduction of unnecessary complexity into their organizations. This approach fosters a culture of adaptability and flexibility, ensuring that organizations remain effective and efficient in the face of ever-changing external demands.

In one example, an executive-level leader sought to improve data collection within their organization by creating a new data entry form to be completed at various sites and locations. The goal was to increase transparency, reduce employee workload, and streamline processes (Bonn, 2023). Much time was spent developing the form and associated processes, followed by extensive employee training and troubleshooting to address initial errors and confusion (Kotter, 1996).

Unfortunately, while the new data entry form and process successfully achieved its intended purpose, nothing from the previous system was removed or replaced (Fullan, 2001). As a result, employees were left with double the workload and faced additional layers of complexity and accountability (Covey, 1989). The time and resources spent creating and implementing the new system ultimately did not simplify the organization's processes or reduce the burden on employees, highlighting the importance of eliminating or replacing existing procedures when introducing new initiatives (Senge, 1990).

This example underscores the critical nature of the principles discussed in this section, emphasizing the need for leaders to focus on simplifying and streamlining systems for success. By carefully considering the potential impacts of new initiatives and ensuring that they replace or eliminate existing processes rather than merely adding complexity, leaders can avoid the pitfalls encountered in this example and create more efficient, effective organizations.

In contrast to the previous example, the executive-level leader could have taken an alternative approach to simplifying and streamlining the data collection process. First, the leader should have conducted a thorough analysis of the existing data collection systems to identify redundancies, inefficiencies, and areas for improvement

(Kotter, 1996). Engaging employees in this process would have allowed them to provide valuable insights and feedback, ensuring that their needs and concerns were addressed (Covey, 1989).

Once the analysis was complete, the leader could have worked with their team to develop a new data entry form and process that would meet the initial goals of increased transparency and reduced workload and directly replace or eliminate existing processes (Senge, 1990). By removing redundant or outdated components of the previous system, the organization could have avoided adding unnecessary complexity and burden on employees (Fullan, 2001).

In the new form and process, the leader should have ensured that employees received adequate training and support to transition to the updated system smoothly. Clear communication and expectations would have been vital in helping employees understand the reasons for the changes and how they would ultimately benefit from the streamlined processes (Kotter, 1996).

Taking these steps, the leader would have successfully simplified the organization's data collection processes and reduced the burden on employees while still achieving the intended goals of increased transparency and efficiency. This approach demonstrates the importance of emphasizing simplicity and clarity in organizational systems to ensure success and minimize unintended consequences (Fullan, 2001).

Case Study: Struggling to Improve Math Achievement in a K-12 Organization

Greenwood School District faced a significant challenge: improving math achievement across all grade levels. For years, the district had struggled to increase student performance in math. Their most recent strategy involved adopting new math textbooks and curricula at the cost of millions of dollars.

The implementation process was complex and time-consuming. First, the district had to train the teaching staff on the new materials and curriculum before implementing them in the classroom. Administrators were then tasked with observing, analyzing, and evaluating the new curriculum's success and comparing student-level data to the previous math curriculum. This process was costly and placed a tremendous burden on teachers and administrators.

Moreover, some teachers were resistant to the new curriculum. They had just achieved proficiency and mastery in the content and teaching strategies of the old math textbook and were familiar with its use in the classroom. These teachers were reluctant to learn a new system and preferred to continue using the previous math textbook.

The district's approach to improving math achievement by adopting new textbooks and curricula proved problematic. The financial investment, the time required for training and implementation, and the resistance from some teachers added layers of complexity and burden to an already struggling organization. The district needed to find a better way to improve math achievement while keeping its systems and processes straightforward and effective.

The process and implementation of new math textbooks and curriculum in Greenwood School District faced several challenges and flaws, ultimately resulting in frustration, anxiety, tension among staff, reluctance, resistance, and adverse effects on morale. The primary flaws in this process and implementation can be attributed to the following factors:

1. Financial burden: The district's decision to invest millions of dollars in new textbooks and curricula placed a significant financial burden on the organization, which could have been allocated to other resources or initiatives to improve math achievement (Fullan, 2007).

2. Time-consuming training and implementation: The time required for training and implementing the new curriculum placed an additional workload on already overburdened teachers and administrators, leading to increased stress and tension (Senge, 1990).

3. Resistance to change: The introduction of the new curriculum was met with resistance from some teachers who had just mastered the previous textbook and were reluctant to learn a new system, thereby hindering the successful adoption of the new curriculum (Kotter, 1996).

4. Lack of focus on the root cause: By focusing solely on adopting new textbooks and curriculum, the district failed to address the underlying factors contributing to low math achievements, such as ineffective teaching strategies, lack of support for struggling students, and inadequate resources (Covey, 2004).

Two researchers, Fullan (2007) and Senge (1990) have provided empirical evidence highlighting the importance of understanding and addressing the root causes of low academic achievement and the need for systemic change rather than simply adopting new curriculum materials. Fullan (2007) argues that sustainable improvement in education requires a focus on capacity-building and developing effective teaching and learning strategies. Similarly, Senge (1990) emphasizes the importance of addressing systemic issues, such as ineffective teaching practices and inadequate resources, to improve educational outcomes.

Understanding the flaws in the new math textbooks and curriculum process and implementation, leaders can learn from these mistakes and work towards adopting more effective and simplified strategies to improve math achievement while minimizing the negative impact on staff morale and reducing resistance to change.

A more effective and simplified approach to improving math achievement in Greenwood School District while adhering to the principle of keeping it vanilla could involve the following strategies:

1. Focus on capacity building and professional development: Instead of investing in new textbooks and curriculum materials, the district could allocate resources to provide teachers with ongoing professional development

opportunities to enhance their math teaching skills and understand effective instructional practices (Darling-Hammond, 2000). This would empower teachers to support their students better and improve math achievement.

2. Implement evidence-based instructional strategies: Encourage the adoption of research-based instructional strategies, such as collaborative learning, problem-solving, and formative assessment techniques, which have been proven to improve student outcomes in math (Hattie, 2009).

3. Support struggling students: Develop targeted interventions and support systems to address the needs of struggling students, such as tutoring programs, differentiated instruction, and individualized learning plans (Slavin, 1996).

4. Foster a culture of continuous improvement: Create a culture within the organization that encourages ongoing reflection, collaboration, and improvement, focusing on student achievement and growth (DuFour, DuFour, Eaker, & Many, 2010).

Implementing these strategies, Greenwood School District can create a simplified and more effective approach to improving math achievement while minimizing the negative impact on staff morale and reducing resistance to change.

Strategies for streamlining processes and eliminating unnecessary bureaucracy.

To streamline processes and eliminate unnecessary bureaucracy within organizations, leaders can adopt several strategies to simplify systems and improve overall effectiveness. By incorporating the Pareto Principle (80/20 rule), focusing on the most impactful issues, and understanding the challenges of change, leaders can create an environment that fosters simplicity and success.

1. Apply the Pareto Principle: The Pareto Principle, also known as the 80/20 rule, states that 80% of the effects come from 20% of the causes. In organizational management, this principle suggests that leaders should identify and focus on the few critical issues that significantly impact organizational performance (Koch, 1999). Leaders can maximize their impact and achieve better results by concentrating their time, effort, and resources on these high-priority areas.

2. Avoid organizational paralysis: To keep systems simple and effective, leaders must be mindful of the potential for organizational paralysis. This can occur when too many layers of bureaucracy, excessive procedures, and complex processes are introduced. To combat this, leaders should regularly assess their organization's processes and identify opportunities for simplification and streamlining (Drucker, 2001).

3. Embrace focused leadership: Many leaders take on too many tasks and initiatives, leading to a lack of focus and diluted impact. To be successful, leaders need to narrow their focus to the most critical and influential issues and dedicate their energy and resources to addressing these priorities with an obsessive-compulsive attitude (Collins, 2001).

4. Understand and manage resistance to change: Change can be challenging for individuals and organizations. Leaders must recognize that resistance to change is a natural human response and work to motivate, inspire, and influence their team members to engage in new concepts, ideas, practices, or procedures (Kotter, 1996). Effective communication, support, and collaboration are essential for navigating the complexities of change and fostering a culture that embraces innovation and growth.

By implementing these strategies, leaders can keep their organizations focused on the most critical priorities, reduce bureaucracy, and promote simplicity and success. As Dr. Christopher Bonn emphasizes, simplicity is the key to success; leaders should always strive to keep it vanilla.

In this Chapter, "Keep it Vanilla - Simplifying Systems for Success," emphasizes the importance of simplicity and clarity in organizational systems. Overcomplicating processes, adding unnecessary layers of bureaucracy, and failing to streamline operations can lead to organizational paralysis, diminished employee morale, increased frustration, anxiety, and tension among staff members. This results in ineffective organizations, inefficiency, subpar performance, and failure.

The chapter discusses case studies demonstrating the effectiveness of simplified systems, highlighting the pitfalls of adding new initiatives, programs, and protocols without considering the impact on existing processes and employee workload. By identifying and addressing the most significant issues and dedicating the majority of time and resources to them, leaders can maximize their impact and foster a culture of simplicity.

Additionally, the chapter explores strategies for streamlining processes and eliminating unnecessary bureaucracy, including applying the Pareto Principle, embracing focused leadership, and managing resistance to change. By understanding the complexities of change and fostering a culture that embraces innovation and growth, leaders can implement simplified systems that contribute to organizational success.

"Keep it Vanilla" underscores the necessity of simplifying systems to enhance organizational effectiveness and efficiency. By avoiding overcomplication and focusing on the most critical aspects of the organization, leaders can create an environment that fosters success, boosts employee morale, and ultimately leads to better performance and results.

Principle 2:
Don't Feed Monsters - Addressing Dysfunctional Dynamics

In this Chapter, "Don't Feed Monsters - Addressing Dysfunctional Dynamics," focuses on addressing dysfunctional behaviors and patterns within an organization. Dysfunctional dynamics can negatively impact an organization's culture, productivity, and overall success. By identifying and addressing toxic behaviors and individuals, leaders can mitigate the detrimental effects of these dynamics and foster a healthier, more effective organization.

This chapter delves into the following sections:

1. Identifying and addressing toxic behaviors and individuals within an organization: The chapter discusses various strategies for recognizing and confronting harmful behaviors and individuals contributing to a dysfunctional work environment. It also covers managing these situations effectively to minimize disruption and promote positive change.

2. Techniques for preventing the development of destructive patterns: Preventing dysfunctional dynamics from taking root in an organization is just as crucial as addressing existing issues. This section explores proactive measures leaders can take to stop destructive patterns before they escalate and adversely affect the organization.

3. Empirical research on the impact of healthy dynamics on organizational success: To underscore the importance of addressing dysfunctional dynamics, this section presents empirical research highlighting the positive impact of healthy relationships and dynamics on an organization's success. The research emphasizes the correlation between effective leadership, a positive work culture, and overall organizational performance.

Chapter 3, "Don't Feed Monsters - Addressing Dysfunctional Dynamics," emphasizes the need to proactively address dysfunctional organizational behaviors and patterns. Leaders can create a supportive and productive work environment that contributes to the organization's overall success by tackling toxic behaviors, preventing destructive patterns, and fostering healthy dynamics.

In organizations, several types of toxic individuals can negatively impact the workplace. These individuals can come from within the organization or from external sources such as media, legislatures, parents, community, and students.

The following are some common types of toxic individuals, along with specific examples and details:

1. Toxic Employees: These individuals often engage in harmful behaviors, such as bullying, gossiping, and undermining colleagues. For example, a toxic employee might spread rumors about a coworker, causing division and mistrust within the team (Pearson & Porath, 2005).

2. Toxic Media: Negative media coverage can damage an organization's reputation and demoralize employees. For example, a news article might sensationalize a minor incident within a school, leading to public outrage and creating undue pressure on the staff (Deephouse, 2000).

3. Toxic Legislatures: Some politicians may introduce legislation that burdens organizations excessively or pushes their agendas. For example, a legislator might propose a bill that imposes strict testing requirements on schools, creating additional stress for teachers and students without addressing the underlying issues (Ravitch, 2016).

4. Toxic Parents: Overbearing or confrontational parents can create tension and conflict within an educational setting. For example, a parent might repeatedly challenge a teacher's

decisions, undermining their authority and causing disruptions in the classroom (Steinberg, 2001).

5. Toxic Community: A hostile or unsupportive community can negatively impact an organization's success. For example, a community might resist a school's efforts to implement inclusive policies, leading to divisions and hampering the school's ability to provide a welcoming environment for all students (Fisher, Frey, & Pumpian, 2012).

6. Toxic Students: Students who exhibit disruptive, disrespectful, or aggressive behaviors can harm the learning environment and create challenges for educators. For example, a student might consistently disrupt class, making it difficult for the teacher to maintain order and effectively teach the material (Skiba, Horner, Chung, Rausch, May, & Tobin, 2011).

7.
Addressing toxic individuals or "monsters" within an organization cannot be overstated. These individuals are driven to disrupt the organization, create fear and havoc among stakeholders, and consume valuable time and energy. Their motives may range from seeking power to expressing their discontent, but their actions invariably negatively affect the organization and its members (Sutton, 2007).

Toxic individuals often begin by attacking the leadership and then move on to the organization. When this strategy fails, they target those loyal or obedient to the leadership. They may even go so far as to attack personal affiliates, such as family, close friends, and former colleagues. When all else fails, they attack character, spreading slander and defamation to ruin reputations (Sutton, 2007).

Despite the challenges posed by toxic individuals, leaders often expend too much time and effort trying to explain, convince, or motivate them. However, the most effective way to deal with these "monsters" is to stop feeding them the attention and validation they crave. By maintaining professionalism and courtesy, leaders can minimize the damage caused by toxic individuals and prevent them from derailing the organization's mission and progress (Sutton, 2007).

Dealing with toxic individuals or "monsters" within an organization is critical to maintaining a healthy and productive work environment. These individuals, driven by various motives, can wreak havoc on an organization and its stakeholders, consuming valuable time and resources.

Leaders must recognize the importance of addressing these issues and not feed the monsters by giving them undue attention or validation. Remaining professional and courteous, leaders can mitigate the damage caused by toxic individuals and ensure the organization stays focused on its mission. With this understanding, the next section will delve into identifying and addressing toxic behaviors and individuals within an organization, providing leaders with the necessary tools to create a more harmonious and effective work environment.

Identifying and addressing toxic behaviors and individuals within an organization

Toxic behaviors and individuals in an organization can create a detrimental environment, negatively impacting the organization's performance, employee morale, and overall success (Bonn, 2023). Leaders must address these issues to foster a supportive and productive work atmosphere. This section will discuss identifying and addressing toxic behaviors and individuals in an organization, integrating relevant empirical research, and providing guidance for leaders.

One of the first steps in addressing toxic behaviors is recognizing the signs. Toxic individuals may exhibit various destructive behaviors, such as manipulation, excessive complaining, blaming others, and undermining colleagues (Porath & Pearson, 2013).

Additionally, they may engage in more covert activities like gossiping, spreading rumors, or sabotaging the work of others (Bonn, 2023).

Empirical research highlights the negative consequences of toxic behavior on organizations. According to a study by Porath and Pearson (2013), toxic behaviors can lead to decreased job satisfaction, increased turnover, and reduced productivity. Moreover, the study found that toxic individuals can harm the overall work climate, eroding trust and collaboration among team members.

To address toxic behaviors, leaders must first confront the individuals responsible. It is essential to approach these conversations with empathy and professionalism, providing clear examples of the problematic behavior and explaining its negative impact on the organization (Bonn, 2023). By addressing the issue directly and assertively, leaders can set expectations for change and convey the importance of a healthy work environment (Lipman, 2016).

In cases where toxic behavior persists despite intervention, leaders may need to consider more drastic measures, such as reassignment, disciplinary action, or termination (Bonn, 2023). Leaders must act decisively and consistently, demonstrating their commitment to maintaining a positive work environment.

Preventative measures can also be vital in mitigating toxic behavior within an organization. By fostering a culture of open communication, transparency, and accountability, leaders can create an environment where toxic behaviors are less likely to thrive (Bonn, 2023). Additionally, regular training and support for employees can help build resilience and promote healthy coping mechanisms, reducing the likelihood of toxic behavior taking root (Porath & Pearson, 2013).

Identifying and addressing toxic behaviors and individuals within an organization is critical for maintaining a healthy and productive work environment. By recognizing the signs, confronting the issue directly, and implementing preventative measures, leaders can cultivate a supportive atmosphere that promotes success and well-being for all organization members.

This case study exemplifies a situation where a toxic individual prevailed, resulting in negative consequences for the entire organization. The lack of effective intervention and the continuous feeding of the rogue teacher's toxic behavior led to the deterioration of the school's culture and the dismissal of a principal who was initially focused on student achievement.

The case of Ms. Johnson and the school illustrates several key failures in the organization's attempts to address the toxic behavior:

1. Lack of a timely intervention: The organization and the principal did not act swiftly to address Ms. Johnson's behavior, allowing her to escalate her attacks against the principal, staff, and eventually the principal's family (Einarsen, Skogstad, Rørvik, Lande, & Nielsen, 2016).

2. Excessive focus on appeasement: The principal and other staff members spent considerable time and effort trying to reconcile with Ms. Johnson despite her continued hostility. This focus on appeasement detracted from their primary responsibilities, such as improving student achievement (Cohen & Blake, 2016).

3. Ineffective communication and conflict resolution: The organization failed to implement effective communication strategies and conflict resolution techniques to address the situation, resulting in further escalation of the conflict (Bacal, 2016).

4. Neglect of core responsibilities: As a result of the ongoing conflict, the focus shifted away from the school's primary mission of providing quality education to its students. This led to academic failure and poor organizational performance,

which eventually resulted in the principal's dismissal (Einarsen et al., 2016).

The organization's failure to effectively address the toxic behavior of Ms. Johnson led to a downward spiral that negatively impacted the entire school. By focusing too much on appeasement and not adequately addressing the underlying issues, the school allowed the toxic behavior to continue and eventually harm the school's primary mission (Cohen & Blake, 2016).

In this revised case study scenario, the principal and the organization effectively apply the principle "Don't feed monsters" to address the toxic behavior of Ms. Johnson:

1. Timely intervention: Upon discovering Ms. Johnson's toxic behavior, the principal and the organization immediately address the issue. They initiate a thorough investigation to gather facts and evidence, ensuring fair and objective decision-making (Bacal, 2016).

2. Prioritizing core responsibilities: Despite the ongoing conflict, the principal and the staff remain focused on their primary responsibilities, such as improving student achievement and maintaining a positive school climate (Cohen & Blake, 2016).

3. Fact-based accountability: The principal and the organization hold Ms. Johnson accountable for her actions based on the evidence gathered during the investigation. They implement appropriate disciplinary measures and establish clear expectations for acceptable behavior in the workplace (Einarsen et al., 2016).

4. Anticipating and preparing for toxic individuals: Recognizing that toxic people will always exist, the principal and the organization develop a proactive game plan to address toxic behaviors. They provide training for staff on

effective communication, conflict resolution, and maintaining a positive work environment (Bacal, 2016).

Following the "Don't feed monsters" principle, the principal and the organization successfully addressed Ms. Johnson's toxic behavior without compromising their focus on the school's primary mission. By setting clear expectations, maintaining accountability, and addressing the issue swiftly, they demonstrate that bullying, harassment, and toxic behaviors will not be tolerated (Cohen & Blake, 2016).

Techniques for preventing the development of destructive patterns.

In this section, we discuss techniques for preventing the development of destructive patterns within organizations. Leaders must understand that they cannot sacrifice their time, energy, attention, resources, or money to appease toxic individuals or monsters. Instead, they should focus on maintaining a healthy organizational culture and addressing toxic behaviors before they become destructive. Todd Whitaker famously said, "The culture of any organization is shaped by the worst behavior the leader is willing to tolerate" (Whitaker et al., 2013).

Keeping this in mind, leaders should adhere to the following principles:

1. Clear communication of expectations: Leaders must be clear and concise in communicating their expectations to employees, outlining the standards for professional behavior and the consequences for failing to comply (Cohen & Blake, 2016).

2. Consistency in enforcing consequences: Leaders must follow through with the established consequences when toxic behavior arises. Consistency in enforcement demonstrates a commitment to maintaining a healthy work environment (Einarsen et al., 2016).

3. Documentation and evidence: Leaders should document any instances of toxic behavior and keep evidence to support their actions. This documentation will be essential in addressing any disputes or challenges that may arise (Bacal, 2016).

4. Remaining calm and composed: Leaders must maintain their composure when dealing with toxic individuals, avoiding emotional reactions that can exacerbate the situation. Staying calm and collected will help leaders navigate these challenging situations more effectively (Cohen & Blake, 2016).

Adhering to these principles, leaders can prevent the development of destructive patterns within their organizations and protect their employees' well-being and overall success.

Dealing with toxic outside stakeholders requires a similar approach to managing toxic employees.

Here are some key points to consider when addressing inappropriate or toxic behavior from external stakeholders:

1. Establish boundaries: Clearly define the limits of interaction with outside stakeholders and communicate those boundaries to ensure everyone understands the expectations for professional conduct (Huang et al., 2020).

2. Maintain professionalism: Always remain professional in interacting with external stakeholders, even when faced with toxic behavior. This approach reinforces the organization's commitment to maintaining a respectful and healthy environment (Cohen & Blake, 2016).

3. Communicate consequences: Make it clear to external stakeholders that inappropriate or toxic behavior will not be tolerated and outline the potential consequences for such actions. Consistent enforcement of these consequences

sends a message that the organization takes these issues seriously (Bacal, 2016).

4. Foster a positive culture: Promote a positive organizational culture that values respect, collaboration, and open communication. This will help reduce the influence of toxic behavior from outside stakeholders (Einarsen et al., 2016).

5. Seek support when needed: If an external stakeholder's toxic behavior persists or escalates, seek support from legal or human resources professionals to ensure the situation is handled appropriately and complies with applicable regulations (Huang et al., 2020).

Following these strategies, organizations can effectively manage toxic behavior from external stakeholders and maintain a positive and productive work environment.

Case Study: Dealing with a Disruptive Parent in a School Setting

Background:

At a local school, an irate mother frequently visits the front office, causing a scene whenever her son is disciplined for violating the student code of conduct. She exhibits aggressive behavior, such as using profanity, refusing to check in at the front office, and shouting obscenities in front of other students. She also threatens staff members interacting with her son, including teachers, school security, the school resource officer, and the principal. This has led to parents removing their children from the school, staff members fleeing the office, and the principal feeling intimidated and unsure of how to handle the situation. The mother often threatens to sue the school and staff, claiming she does not need permission to enter the school because she pays taxes. Her son's behavior has also escalated as he mimics his mother's actions.

Solution Using Chapter 3 Model:

1. Establish boundaries: The school should communicate its policies and expectations for parent behavior when on school grounds. This may include implementing a check-in process for all visitors, outlining appropriate behavior, and setting consequences for violating these policies (Huang et al., 2020).

2. Maintain professionalism: The school staff, including the principal, should remain calm and professional during interactions with the disruptive parent. They should avoid engaging in arguments or responding to provocations and instead focus on the student's best interests (Cohen & Blake, 2016).

3. Communicate consequences: The principal should inform the disruptive parent of the consequences for continuing her inappropriate behavior. This may include restricting her access to the school or involving law enforcement if necessary (Bacal, 2016).

4. Foster a positive culture: The school should continue to promote a positive environment by reinforcing respectful behavior among all members of the school community, including staff, students, and parents (Einarsen et al., 2016).

5. Seek support when needed: If the disruptive parent's behavior persists or escalates, the principal should seek guidance from legal or human resources professionals to ensure the situation is handled appropriately and in accordance with any applicable regulations (Huang et al., 2020).

Implementing these strategies, the school can effectively address the disruptive behavior of the irate parent, maintain a positive and safe environment for students and staff, and prevent further disruptions from negatively impacting the school community.

By setting boundaries, maintaining professionalism, communicating consequences, fostering a positive culture, and seeking support when needed, the school can overcome the challenges posed by the disruptive parent and focus on improving student achievement and overall school performance.

Empirical research on the impact of healthy dynamics on organizational success

Fostering a healthy organizational culture and effectively managing toxic individuals cannot be overstated. As Todd Whitaker, an expert in the field of education leadership, points out in his book, "Dealing with Difficult Teachers" (Whitaker, 2002), toxic individuals can have a detrimental impact on the overall culture and climate of an organization. They consume valuable time and energy that should be spent on improving the organization's performance and meeting goals and objectives. Moreover, they often tarnish the organization's and its members' image and credibility.

Whitaker emphasizes that leaders must take a proactive approach to creating a positive work environment, as it is crucial to the success of any organization. In his book, "What Great Principals Do Differently" (Whitaker, 2012), he highlights the importance of leaders focusing on the most effective staff members and supporting their growth and development. By doing so, they can create a positive ripple effect throughout the organization, raising the overall level of performance and contributing to a healthier work culture.

A study by Porath and Pearson (2012) found that exposure to incivility in the workplace led to decreased productivity, increased turnover, and a negative impact on employee well-being. The study demonstrates the importance of maintaining a positive work environment and addressing toxic behaviors that undermine organizational success.

Similarly, a study by Barsade and O'Neill (2014) showed that a positive work environment, characterized by a supportive and respectful culture, contributes to higher levels of employee engagement, increased job satisfaction, and better performance. This research underscores leaders' critical role in creating and sustaining a healthy organizational culture.

Empirical research demonstrates the significant impact that healthy dynamics have on organizational success. By effectively managing toxic individuals and fostering a positive work culture, leaders can enhance employee well-being, improve performance, and achieve the organization's goals and objectives.

It is crucial for leaders to recognize the importance of addressing toxic behaviors and to develop strategies to maintain a supportive and respectful work environment for all members of the organization.

Fostering a healthy organizational culture and effectively managing toxic individuals are crucial to successful leadership. As Todd Whitaker's work and various empirical studies have shown, toxic people can significantly hinder an organization's success by consuming valuable time and energy, damaging the work environment, and tarnishing the organization's and its members' credibility.

By focusing on maintaining a positive work culture and addressing toxic behaviors proactively, leaders can enhance employee well-being, improve performance, and achieve their organization's goals and objectives. Leaders need to recognize the importance of these factors and develop strategies to create a supportive and respectful work environment for all members of the organization.

Applying the principles outlined in this chapter, leaders can effectively address toxic individuals and create an environment where their organization can thrive. By keeping it simple, not feeding monsters, and promoting healthy dynamics, leaders can ensure that their organization remains successful, efficient, and a positive workplace.

Case Study: Smith & Co. - A Tale of Organizational Transformation

Smith & Co. was a medium-sized manufacturing company experiencing a decline in productivity and employee morale due to toxic individuals and dysfunctional organizational dynamics. The company's leadership team implemented the principles outlined in Chapter 3, "Don't Feed Monsters - Addressing Dysfunctional Dynamics," to turn the situation around.

Step 1: Identifying Toxic Individuals and Behaviors The company's leadership team began by identifying toxic individuals and behaviors within the organization. Several employees were gossiping, spreading negativity, and undermining colleagues' efforts. These individuals created a toxic environment, hindering collaboration and stifling innovation.

Step 2: Addressing Toxic Behaviors and Individuals The leadership team swiftly addressed the identified toxic behaviors and individuals. They held one-on-one meetings with the problematic employees, clearly communicating their expectations and the consequences of continued toxic behavior. The leaders documented these conversations and supported employees in improving their behavior. They also clarified that further disciplinary action would be taken if improvement did not occur.

Step 3: Preventing the Development of Destructive Patterns To prevent destructive patterns from emerging, the company's leadership team implemented regular training sessions on effective communication, teamwork, and conflict resolution. They also encouraged open dialogue and created a confidential reporting system for employees to report toxic behaviors or concerns without fear of retaliation.

Step 4: Fostering Healthy Dynamics and Organizational Success With the toxic behaviors addressed and preventive measures in place, Smith & Co. experienced a remarkable transformation. Employees began to feel more supported, and the work environment became more positive and collaborative. As a result, the company saw a significant increase in productivity and employee morale.

Following the principles outlined in this chapter, Smith & Co. successfully addressed their toxic individuals and dysfunctional dynamics, ultimately leading to a healthier, more successful organization. This case study exemplifies how implementing the "Don't Feed Monsters" principle with fidelity can lead to organizational success.

In "Don't Feed Monsters - Addressing Dysfunctional Dynamics," we explored the importance of addressing toxic behaviors and individuals within an organization. Leaders can prevent destructive patterns from developing and maintaining a healthy organizational culture by identifying and addressing toxic behaviors.

The chapter began by examining the various types of toxic individuals in organizations, both internal and external and their potential impact on the work environment. We discussed the importance of addressing toxic individuals and keeping them from consuming valuable time, energy, and resources. Using real-life examples and empirical research, we demonstrated the negative consequences of allowing toxic individuals to disrupt and damage an organization.

Next, we presented strategies for effectively dealing with toxic individuals, emphasizing the need to remain professional, courteous, and fact-based. We illustrated the importance of not feeding monsters by providing a framework for addressing toxic individuals and maintaining focus on the organization's goals and objectives.

Additionally, we discussed techniques for preventing the development of destructive patterns, highlighting the need for clear communication of expectations and consequences, documentation, and remaining calm and collected. The chapter concluded by exploring the impact of healthy dynamics on organizational success, drawing on the work of Todd Whitaker and empirical research to emphasize the importance of fostering a positive work culture.

This chapter provided valuable insights and strategies for leaders to effectively address and manage toxic behaviors and individuals in their organizations. Understanding the importance of maintaining healthy dynamics and not feeding monsters, leaders can create a supportive and successful work environment for their teams.

Principle 3:
Water Flowers, Not Weeds - Nurturing Talent and Growth

Every organization is like a vibrant garden with unique and diverse talents waiting to bloom. As a leader, the role resembles that of a master gardener: watering the flowers, not the weeds. Focusing on nurturing talent and growth, create an environment where people can flourish and reach their full potential. This principle is about celebrating team accomplishments, using ceremonies and recognition to inspire, motivate, and foster organizational loyalty. It is time to have some fun and lighten the mood because who does not love a good garden party?

This delightful chapter will explore three key sections that support this principle. First, learn how to recognize and foster potential within an organization. Much like how a skilled gardener can spot a good sapling, discover how to identify the budding talents within the team, and help them grow.

Next, delve into strategies for developing a growth mindset and supporting professional development. Examine how to cultivate a rich learning environment that encourages growth, just as the suitable soil and nutrients help a garden to thrive. Get ready to roll up your sleeves and dig into personal and professional development.

Finally, discuss the role of effective performance management systems in promoting growth. After all, a well-tended garden requires regular pruning and care. Explore how to design performance management systems that support the growth and success of team members, keeping the organizational garden vibrant and healthy.

This chapter draws on the wisdom of renowned educators and authors on organizational leadership. Incorporating the insights and expertise of these esteemed researchers will guide me on this journey of nurturing talent and growth within the organization.

Together, we will discover the secrets to creating a flourishing garden of success where team members can blossom and thrive. So, grab gardening gloves and get started on this fun and engaging adventure in cultivating an environment that fosters the growth and development of the team!

Recognizing and Fostering Potential Within an Organization Introduction

Every organization is like a vibrant garden with unique and diverse talents waiting to bloom. As a leader, the role resembles that of a master gardener: watering the flowers, not the weeds. Focusing on nurturing talent and growth, create an environment where people can flourish and reach their full potential. This principle is about celebrating team accomplishments, using ceremonies and recognition to inspire, motivate, and foster organizational loyalty. It is time to have some fun and lighten the mood because who does not love a good garden party?

Identifying and Cultivating Budding Talents

To foster talent and growth within an organization, it is essential to recognize and nurture the potential of team members. Much like a skilled gardener can spot a good sapling, leaders must develop the ability to identify budding talents within the team and provide them with the support and opportunities to grow. This involves creating a culture of trust and open communication where employees feel comfortable showcasing their skills and aspirations. By leveraging tools such as talent assessments, mentorship programs, and performance evaluations, leaders can identify individuals who exhibit promising qualities and provide tailored development plans to help them thrive (Serge, 2022).

Cultivating a Growth Mindset and Embracing Professional Development

A key aspect of nurturing talent and growth is cultivating a growth mindset within the organization. Like how suitable soil and nutrients help a garden thrive, leaders must create a rich learning environment that encourages continuous development. By promoting a culture of learning, offering training programs, and providing access to resources, employees are empowered to expand their knowledge and skills. This fosters personal and professional growth, enabling individuals to contribute to the organization's success and reach their full potential (Whitaker, 2021).

Designing Effective Performance Management Systems for Growth

Just as a well-tended garden requires regular pruning and care, an organization's performance management systems are crucial in promoting growth. Effective performance management involves setting clear expectations, providing constructive feedback, and offering opportunities for improvement and advancement. By aligning individual goals with organizational objectives, leaders can create a supportive framework that encourages continuous growth and development (Fullan, 2020). Through regular performance evaluations, coaching, and mentorship, team members can enhance their skills, overcome challenges, and thrive in their roles.

Drawing on the insights of esteemed educators and authors on organizational leadership, such as Dr. Peter Serge, Dr. Todd Whitaker, Dr. Michael Fullan, and Dr. Stephen Covey, this chapter explores the importance of recognizing and fostering potential within an organization. By implementing strategies to identify budding talents, cultivating a growth mindset, and designing effective performance management systems, leaders can create an environment that nurtures talent and enables individuals to reach their full potential. Together, we embark on this journey of creating a flourishing garden of success where team members can blossom and thrive (Covey, 2021).

Recognizing and Fostering Potential Within an Organization - A Case Study

Recognizing and fostering potential within an organization is crucial for creating a thriving environment where individuals can grow and excel. This case study demonstrates how ABC Corporation implemented strategies to identify and nurture talent, cultivate a growth mindset, and design effective performance management systems. Embracing these principles, ABC Corporation experienced a transformative individual and organizational growth journey.

Identifying and Cultivating Budding Talents

At ABC Corporation, leaders recognized the importance of identifying and nurturing talented individuals. They implemented a talent assessment program to identify employees with exceptional skills and potential. The organization identified a group of high-potential employees through a comprehensive evaluation process, including performance evaluations and feedback from peers and supervisors.

These identified individuals were provided with tailored development plans, including mentorship opportunities and specialized training programs. The organization encouraged an open, transparent culture where employees felt comfortable showcasing their skills and aspirations. ABC Corporation witnessed its growth and contributions flourish by providing these budding talents with the necessary support and opportunities.

Cultivating a Growth Mindset and Embracing Professional Development

ABC Corporation created a learning culture that emphasized continuous development and innovation to foster a growth mindset within the organization. The company offered a wide range of training programs, both internally and externally, to enhance employees' knowledge and skills. These programs focused on leadership, technical expertise, and industry trends.

Additionally, ABC Corporation established knowledge-sharing platforms and communities to encourage peer collaboration and learning. The organization celebrated curiosity, experimentation, and the pursuit of new ideas. Through these initiatives, employees developed a growth mindset and embraced professional development as an ongoing journey of learning and improvement.

Designing Effective Performance Management Systems for Growth

ABC Corporation understood the importance of designing effective performance management systems to support growth. The organization implemented a comprehensive performance evaluation process that aligned individual goals with the company's strategic objectives. Clear expectations were set, and regular feedback was provided to employees.

The performance management system emphasized both recognition and areas for improvement. Employees were encouraged to enhance their skills and overcome challenges through constructive feedback, coaching, and mentorship. ABC Corporation provided opportunities for career advancement, enabling individuals to take on new responsibilities and grow within the organization.

Implementing strategies to recognize and foster potential within the organization, ABC Corporation created an environment where individuals could thrive and reach their full potential. The company's commitment to identifying talent, cultivating a growth mindset, and designing effective performance management systems transformed the organization.

Through these efforts, ABC Corporation experienced increased employee engagement, enhanced performance, and a continuous learning and development culture. By embracing the wisdom of esteemed authors and educators, such as Dr. Peter Serge, Dr. Todd Whitaker, Dr. Michael Fullan, and Dr. Stephen Covey, ABC Corporation became a flourishing garden of success where team members blossomed and thrived (Covey, 2021). This case study serves as a testament to the power of recognizing and fostering potential within an organization for long-term growth and success.

Strategies for Developing a Growth Mindset and Supporting Professional Development

In order to create an environment that fosters talent and growth, leaders must emphasize the importance of developing a growth mindset and supporting the professional development of their team members. Just as suitable soil and nutrients help a garden thrive, cultivating a growth mindset and providing opportunities for continuous learning and development is essential for individuals to reach their full potential. This section explores strategies leaders can employ to nurture a growth mindset and promote ongoing professional growth within their organization.

Cultivating a Learning Culture

Leaders play a vital role in creating a learning culture within the organization. By encouraging a mindset that values curiosity, experimentation, and continuous learning, leaders can inspire their team members to embrace new challenges and expand their knowledge and skills. This can be achieved through various initiatives, such as establishing learning communities, hosting regular knowledge-sharing sessions, and providing access to relevant resources and training programs. Fostering a culture that celebrates learning and growth, leaders empower their team members to develop and apply new skills, enhancing performance and increasing job satisfaction (Dweck, 2006).

Setting Clear Goals and Providing Feedback

Leaders should set clear goals and expectations for their team members to support professional development. Leaders align individual goals with organizational objectives and create a framework that promotes growth and development. Regular feedback and performance evaluations are essential to this strategy, as they provide valuable insights for improvement and allow individuals to track their progress. Constructive feedback and opportunities for recognition and celebration of achievements encourage individuals to develop a growth mindset and continuously strive for excellence (Grant & Dweck, 2003).

Encouraging Collaboration and Mentoring

Collaboration and mentoring are powerful tools for fostering professional growth. Leaders create an environment that values collective learning and growth by encouraging team members to collaborate on projects, share knowledge, and learn from one another's expertise. Mentoring programs, both formal and informal, enable experienced individuals to guide and support the development of their colleagues, providing valuable insights, advice, and encouragement. Through these collaborative efforts, team members can expand their skill sets, gain new perspectives, and build meaningful professional relationships (Ragins & Verbos, 2007).

Providing Development Opportunities

Leaders can support professional development by offering a range of opportunities for skill-building and career advancement. This can include workshops, seminars, conferences, and certifications relevant to their team members' roles and aspirations. By investing in the growth and development of their employees, leaders demonstrate a commitment to their success and create a sense of loyalty and engagement within the organization. Additionally, providing stretch assignments and opportunities for individuals to take on new responsibilities can challenge and motivate team members, fostering their professional growth and preparing them for future leadership roles (Laker & Powell, 2011).

By implementing strategies to develop a growth mindset and support professional development, leaders can create an environment that encourages continuous learning, skill enhancement, and career growth within their organization. Cultivating a learning culture, setting clear goals, providing feedback, encouraging collaboration and mentoring, and offering development opportunities are critical components of this approach. By embracing these strategies, leaders enable their team members to unlock their full potential and contribute to the organization's success.

The Role of Effective Performance Management Systems in Promoting Growth

Just as a well-tended garden requires regular pruning and care, an organization's performance management systems are crucial in promoting growth. By implementing effective performance management practices, leaders can create an environment that supports the development and success of their team members. This section explores how designing and implementing robust performance management systems contribute to fostering talent and growth within an organization.

Setting Clear Expectations

One fundamental aspect of effective performance management is setting clear expectations. When leaders establish specific, measurable, achievable, relevant, and time-bound (SMART) goals, they provide a framework for employees to understand what is expected of them (Locke & Latham, 2019). Clear expectations guide employees to focus their efforts, align their work with organizational objectives, and facilitate personal and professional growth.

Providing Constructive Feedback

Constructive feedback is a valuable tool for fostering growth and development. By offering timely, specific, and actionable feedback, leaders empower their employees to understand their strengths and areas for improvement (London & Smither, 2021). Feedback should be given in a supportive and constructive manner, highlighting achievements and offering guidance on areas that require development. This enables employees to make targeted improvements, enhance their skills, and reach their full potential.

Offering Opportunities for Improvement and Advancement

A key component of effective performance management systems is providing opportunities for improvement and advancement. Leaders should create a supportive environment that encourages employees to seek growth and pursue professional development opportunities. This can include offering training programs, mentoring relationships, job rotations, and stretch assignments (Keller, 2020). By investing in the growth of their employees, organizations foster a culture of continuous improvement and provide avenues for advancement within the company.

Recognizing and Rewarding Achievement

Recognizing and rewarding achievement is a powerful motivator for promoting growth. Effective performance management systems include mechanisms for acknowledging and celebrating employees' accomplishments (Cerasoli et al., 2014). This can take the form of verbal recognition, written appreciation, performance-based bonuses, or career advancement opportunities. By recognizing and rewarding high performance, leaders create a positive and motivating work environment that encourages ongoing growth and excellence.

Designing and implementing effective performance management systems is essential for promoting organizational growth. Leaders create an environment that supports their team members' continuous development and success by setting clear expectations, providing constructive feedback, offering opportunities for improvement and advancement, and recognizing and rewarding achievement. Together, these components form a robust performance management framework that fosters talent and cultivates a culture of growth and excellence within the organization.

Cultivating Success: The Transformation of Team Dynamics at TechCorp - A Case Study

TechCorp, a leading technology company in the Fortune 500, faced a challenging period marked by low employee morale, high turnover rates, and stagnant growth. Recognizing the need for change, the executive leadership implemented a comprehensive approach to nurture talent and promote growth within the organization.

Background

TechCorp had long been known for its focus on technical expertise but neglected the importance of fostering a supportive and growth-oriented culture. The leadership realized that the key to turning things around was to shift the focus from watering the weeds to watering the flowers.

Identifying and Cultivating Budding Talents

TechCorp initiated a talent assessment program aimed at identifying employees with untapped potential. Through skill evaluations, performance reviews, and feedback sessions, managers identified individuals who exhibited exceptional skills, leadership qualities, and a willingness to learn and grow. These talented individuals were then provided with tailored development plans, mentorship opportunities, and additional training to help them maximize their potential.

Cultivating a Growth Mindset and Embracing Professional Development

TechCorp invested in creating a rich learning environment to foster a growth mindset. They implemented a robust professional development program that offered various training courses, workshops, and online resources. Employees were encouraged to take ownership of their growth by setting personal development goals and seeking opportunities for continuous learning. The organization also promoted a culture of collaboration and knowledge sharing, allowing employees to tap into the collective wisdom of their peers.

Designing Effective Performance Management Systems for Growth

TechCorp revamped its performance management systems to align individual goals with its objectives. They introduced a regular mechanism emphasizing constructive feedback, coaching, and mentoring. Performance evaluations became a collaborative process, focusing on past achievements and identifying areas for improvement and growth. This approach made employees feel supported, recognized for their accomplishments, and motivated to reach new heights.

Results and Impact

Implementing the talent nurturing and growth-promoting strategies yielded significant positive outcomes for TechCorp. Employee morale improved, leading to a substantial reduction in turnover rates. The organization witnessed a surge in innovation and creativity as employees felt empowered to contribute ideas and take risks. This newfound enthusiasm translated into increased productivity, enhanced quality of work, and improved customer satisfaction.

TechCorp's organizational culture underwent a remarkable transformation. The emphasis on nurturing talent and fostering growth created employees' sense of belonging and loyalty. The company became known for its supportive and collaborative work environment, attracting top talent and becoming an employer of choice.

The case of TechCorp demonstrates the transformative power of nurturing talent and promoting growth within an organization. Identifying and cultivating budding talents, embracing a growth mindset, and designing effective performance management systems, TechCorp was able to revitalize its organizational culture, drive innovation, and achieve remarkable success. This case serves as a testament to the importance of watering the flowers and investing in the growth and development of employees for long-term organizational prosperity.

In this chapter, we explored the vital principle of nurturing talent and growth within organizations, drawing inspiration from the analogy of a vibrant garden. The chapter emphasized the role of leaders as master gardeners, responsible for creating an environment where individuals can flourish and reach their full potential.

The chapter was divided into three sections, each addressing a crucial aspect of nurturing talent and growth. Recognizing and fostering potential within an organization focused on identifying and cultivating budding talents. By leveraging talent assessments, mentorship programs, and performance evaluations, leaders can recognize individuals with promising qualities and provide them with tailored development plans to help them thrive.

The section Strategies for Developing a growth mindset and supporting professional development delved into cultivating and supporting a growth mindset. Creating a learning culture, offering training programs, and providing access to resources enable employees to expand their knowledge and skills, fostering personal and professional growth.

The role of effective performance management systems in promoting growth highlighted the role of effective performance management systems in promoting growth. Clear expectations, constructive feedback, and opportunities for improvement and advancement contribute to a supportive framework where individuals can continuously grow and succeed.
Throughout the chapter, the insights and expertise of renowned educators and authors on organizational leadership, such as Dr. Peter Serge, Dr. Todd Whitaker, Dr. Michael Fullan, and Dr. Stephen Covey, were drawn upon to guide the journey of nurturing talent and growth.

The chapter emphasized the importance of celebrating team accomplishments using ceremonies and recognition to inspire and foster organizational loyalty. Leaders create a flourishing garden of success where team members can blossom and thrive by watering the flowers and not the weeds.

Through the principles discussed in this chapter, organizations can create an environment that supports talent development, cultivates a growth mindset, and fosters a culture of continuous growth and success. By embracing these practices, leaders can transform their organizations into thriving and innovative spaces where employees can reach their full potential.

Principle 4:
You are PR - Crafting a Positive Organizational Image

In today's interconnected world, the image and reputation of an organization are paramount to its success. Every interaction, every word spoken, and every experience shared by employees and customers becomes a part of the organization's brand. Remembering this when expressing frustrations or negative sentiments about the organization, its clients, customers, or employees is crucial.

In this chapter, we will explore the importance of crafting a positive organizational image and its impact on the perception of competence, toxicity, functionality, and success. The public, whether customers, clients, or the broader community, is not always compassionate or empathetic when judging an organization. Negative comments or complaints can quickly spread and shape the public's perception of the organization as incompetent, toxic, dysfunctional, or failing. To protect the organization's reputation, it is vital to remember that employees, the work environment, public relations efforts, and the relationships with clients and customers all contribute to the organization's overall image.

This chapter will emphasize the need to highlight and accentuate the organization's ability to overcome adversity, persevere, and celebrate even the most minor and short-term successes. By focusing on these positive aspects, leaders can shape a narrative that showcases the organization's strengths, resilience, and dedication to excellence.

We will delve into strategies for crafting a positive organizational image, including effective communication practices, fostering a culture of positivity and transparency, and nurturing strong relationships with clients, customers, and employees. Embracing these principles, leaders can influence the organization's perception, build trust and loyalty, and create a positive brand that resonates with the public.

Throughout this chapter, we will draw upon the wisdom of esteemed public relations, organizational psychology, and leadership experts to provide insights and practical guidance. By adopting the mindset that "You are PR," leaders can actively contribute to shaping a positive and impactful organizational image that sets the stage for continued success.

Join us on this journey of understanding the power of perception, harnessing the potential of positive communication, and crafting a compelling organizational image that leaves a lasting impression on clients, customers, and the wider community. Let us explore the strategies and principles that will enable your organization to thrive in the eyes of the public.

Case Study: The Impact of Negative Leadership at Stride Athletics

This case study examines the repercussions of harmful leadership practices within Stride Athletics, a professional athletic team. The leaders of Stride Athletics consistently complained, blamed athletes for failures, and expressed dissatisfaction with their performance and work ethic. However, this approach had the opposite effect, leading to a toxic team environment and a negative perception of the organization. This case study highlights the importance of promoting, celebrating, and sharing positive information to foster a healthy and prosperous team culture at Stride Athletics.

Once known for its strong team spirit and positive culture, Stride Athletics experienced a significant shift in leadership dynamics when new leaders joined the organization. These leaders adopted a management style that focused on blaming athletes for the team's shortcomings rather than fostering collective responsibility. As a result, negativity and demoralization began to permeate the team, leading to a decline in morale, decreased performance, and a strained team atmosphere.

Negative Leadership's Impact on Athletes

As the leaders consistently blamed and complained about the athletes, a culture of blame and negativity emerged within Stride Athletics. Athletes felt demotivated, undervalued, and disengaged, decreasing performance and team cohesion. The lack of support and encouragement from leadership created a toxic environment, where athletes began mirroring the blaming behavior and expressing frustration with their teammates.

The Ripple Effect on Fans and Sponsors

The hostile atmosphere within Stride Athletics didn't remain contained within the team. As athletes internalized the blaming behavior, it reflected in their interactions with fans and sponsors. Instead of showcasing their skills and building positive relationships, athletes blamed fans and sponsors for their perceived failures. This shift in attitude resulted in a decline in fan engagement, sponsor support, and the overall reputation of Stride Athletics.

The Importance of Promoting Positivity and Celebrating Success

This case study underscores the significance of promoting, celebrating, and sharing positive information within Stride Athletics. Leaders must recognize their words and actions' immense influence on shaping the team's culture and perception. By highlighting successes, acknowledging athlete efforts, and fostering a culture of positivity, leaders can inspire and motivate athletes, creating a more cohesive and high-performing team.

Rebuilding Team Culture

To address the adverse effects of the leadership's behavior, Stride Athletics implemented a comprehensive approach to rebuilding the team culture. This involved introducing programs focused on fostering a positive team environment, improving communication and collaboration, and promoting a culture of accountability and celebration. Additionally, leaders are committed to modeling positive behavior and providing regular opportunities to acknowledge individual and team achievements.

The Resulting Transformation

Over time, Stride Athletics witnessed a remarkable transformation. As leaders focused on promoting positivity and celebrating success, athlete morale improved, and a renewed sense of unity and teamwork emerged. With a renewed emphasis on delivering exceptional performances and building positive relationships with fans and sponsors, Stride Athletics regained its reputation as a respected and admired professional athletic team.

This case study highlights the detrimental effects of harmful leadership practices within Stride Athletics. Leaders can create a healthy and prosperous team culture by recognizing the power of promoting, celebrating, and sharing positive information. Emphasizing positivity, acknowledging athlete efforts, and fostering a culture of accountability can contribute to a motivated and cohesive team, resulting in increased fan engagement, sponsor support, and long-term success for Stride Athletics.

The Significance of a Strong Organizational Brand and Public Image

An organization's overall success and longevity are deeply intertwined with its brand and public image. These perceptions shape the attitudes and beliefs of internal stakeholders—employees, managers, and shareholders—and external stakeholders—customers, clients, competitors, and the broader community (Keller, 2013). The power of these perceptions can act as a catalyst for organizational growth, but they can also trigger a decline if managed ineffectively.

An organization's brand and public image extend beyond just logos or taglines. They embody the organization's core values, mission, and culture (Aaker, 2010). A strong and positive brand image implies competence, quality, and reliability, assuring customers that the organization is capable of fulfilling its promises. A positive public image attracts and retains talent, as employees often aspire to be associated with respected and admired organizations (Cable & Turban, 2003).

In challenging times, a strong organizational brand can serve as a guidepost that directs the organization toward its objectives. It can promote resilience, encouraging employees to persevere and invent creative solutions to challenges (Linnenluecke, 2017). Additionally, a positive public image can offer protection against negative press or public sentiment, assisting the organization in navigating crises with minimal damage to its reputation (Coombs, 2007).

Establishing a solid organizational brand and a positive public image demands active, positive leadership practices. Leaders should celebrate achievements, regardless of their size, and utilize these successes to construct a narrative of resilience and dedication to excellence (Bennis, 2009). A focus on promoting positivity, acknowledging efforts, and celebrating success can transform an organization's culture, leading to enhanced morale and performance (Amabile & Kramer, 2011).

The value of a solid organizational brand and public image is indomitable. It influences everything from internal team dynamics to relationships with customers, clients, and the wider community. Leaders, recognizing and embracing their role in shaping this image and brand, can foster a positive organizational culture that resonates with all stakeholders, paving the path for long-term success.

Best Practices for Effective Communication and Public Relations Strategies

A positive organizational image requires robust and effective communication and public relations strategies. A communication strategy is more than just the means of conveying messages; it embodies the essence of an organization and projects its mission,

vision, and values to its public (Barker, 2008). On the other hand, public relations involves managing relationships with the public to create and maintain a positive reputation (Grunig, 2013). Hence, they play a crucial role in crafting a positive organizational image. Building Trust through Open and Transparent Communication
Open and transparent communication is pivotal to building trust within and with the external public. When communication is open, it promotes a sense of unity and togetherness among employees and fosters a culture of trust and respect (Men, 2014). Conversely, transparency is being open about the organization's activities, decisions, and policies. It reinforces the organization's credibility, creating a sense of trust and enhancing its reputation (Rawlins, 2008).

Regular and Consistent Messaging

Regular and consistent communication is critical to effective public relations. A constant flow of communication helps keep the public informed about the organization's activities, decisions, and policies. Consistency in messaging reinforces the organization's brand and creates a solid and memorable image in the public's minds (Aaker, 2012).

Engaging with the Public

Engaging with the public is a critical aspect of public relations. Engagement allows an organization to build strong relationships with its public and foster a sense of community. It involves listening to the public's concerns, responding to their queries, and involving them in the organization's activities and decision-making process (Kent & Taylor, 2002). An organization can enhance its reputation, increase loyalty, and promote a positive image by engaging with the public.

Crisis Management

How an organization handles a crisis can significantly impact its image and reputation. Effective crisis management involves quick and transparent communication, taking responsibility, and implementing corrective actions. It helps maintain public trust, mitigate damage to the organization's reputation, and even turn a crisis into an opportunity to demonstrate its resilience and commitment to its stakeholders (Coombs, 2007).

Leveraging Digital Platforms

Digital platforms provide an excellent opportunity for organizations to connect with their public. Organizations can utilize social media, blogs, and websites to share updates, promote their brand, and engage with the public. Digital platforms offer a unique opportunity for real-time engagement, allowing organizations to respond quickly to queries, feedback, and criticisms and manage their online reputation (Kietzmann et al., 2011).

Evaluating Communication and PR Efforts

Evaluating the effectiveness of communication and PR efforts is crucial to ensure they achieve the desired results. This can be done through surveys, focus groups, and social media analytics. Feedback from these evaluations can help refine strategies, address issues, and continuously improve communication and PR practices (Watson & Noble, 2007).

A positive organizational image involves much more than having a good product or service. It requires an effective communication and public relations strategy that promotes trust, ensures consistency, encourages engagement, handles crises effectively, leverages digital platforms, and constantly evaluates and improves. When implemented correctly, these practices can help organizations project a positive image, build a strong reputation, and achieve success in the long term.

Case Studies Illustrating the Impact of a Positive Image on Organizational Success

The importance of maintaining a solid brand and a positive public image can be better understood through real-world case studies. These case studies offer insights into the impact of positive branding and public image on organizational success.

Case Study 1: Starbucks - Fostering a Positive Image through Social Responsibility

Starbucks, a multinational coffeehouse chain, has cultivated a positive public image through its commitment to social responsibility. The company's comprehensive Corporate Social Responsibility (CSR) program addresses ethical sourcing, environmental stewardship, and community involvement. Its "Shared Planet" initiative aims to make Starbucks the world's leading purchaser of fair-trade coffee, reduce its environmental footprint, and actively give back to communities (Starbucks, 2020). Promoting these CSR activities, Starbucks successfully portrays itself as a socially responsible corporation, fostering a positive brand image that resonates with consumers (Marques & Lee, 2011).

Case Study 2: Apple - Crafting a Positive Brand Image Through Innovation

The multinational technology company Apple has built a strong brand image through its commitment to innovation. Consistently introducing groundbreaking products and staying ahead of technological trends, Apple has developed a reputation for being a leading innovator in the tech industry. This positive image has attracted loyal customers and driven the organization's financial success (Keller & Lehmann, 2006).

Case Study 3: Patagonia - Strengthening Brand Image through Environmental Advocacy

Patagonia, an outdoor clothing brand, has enhanced its image by actively advocating for environmental sustainability. The company's "1% for the Planet" initiative, where it pledges to donate 1% of its sales to environmental causes, resonates with customers and aligns with the company's mission of building the best product, causing no unnecessary harm, and using business to inspire solutions to the environmental crisis (Patagonia, 2020). This commitment to environmental advocacy strengthens Patagonia's brand image, attracts like-minded consumers, and contributes to its organizational success (Luo & Bhattacharya, 2009).

Case Study 4: Tesla - Shaping a Positive Image through Visionary Leadership

Tesla, a leader in the electric vehicle industry, has created a positive brand image through the visionary leadership of its CEO, Elon Musk. Musk's forward-thinking approach and his commitment to mainstream electric vehicles have revolutionized the automobile industry and positioned Tesla as a progressive and innovative company. This positive image has attracted a strong customer base and boosted the company's success (Hitt et al., 2020).

In this dynamic and interconnected world, organizations are defined not just by their products or services but by their reputation and public image. Our discussion in this chapter underscores the grave repercussions of negative attitudes, constant blaming, and lack of empathy within an organization. Such behaviors have been shown to breed a culture of toxicity, demoralization, and dysfunction, which can significantly damage an organization's public image and success.

The organizational ecosystem rarely offers the sanctuary of compassion, empathy, and mercy. Negative news about an organization can swiftly gain momentum, overshadowing its achievements and poisoning the public's perception. As the case of Stride Athletics demonstrates, consistent complaints, blaming, and dissatisfaction can lead to a toxic environment that affects the internal dynamics and spills over into the organization's interactions with clients, customers, and the wider community.

However, the principles outlined in this chapter offer a beacon of hope. Grounded in empirical research, they provide a blueprint for cultivating a positive organizational image that can withstand adversities, overcome challenges, and celebrate successes, no matter how minor. Effective communication, nurturing a culture of positivity and transparency, and building robust relationships with all stakeholders are the bedrock of these principles. These strategies foster a healthy internal environment and project a compelling image to the outside world, resonating with the public and strengthening the organization's brand.

The case studies of Starbucks, Apple, Patagonia, and Tesla have proven how these principles can be implemented positively. Through their commitment to innovation, social responsibility, environmental advocacy, and visionary leadership, these organizations have successfully managed to create a strong and positive organizational image that has translated into tangible success.

Fostering a positive organizational image is not an optional but a vital exercise for organizations to thrive in today's competitive world. By emphasizing positivity, acknowledging efforts, and fostering a culture of accountability, organizations can navigate the challenges that come their way and emerge stronger. If adopted and implemented, the principles discussed in this chapter can guide organizations on their journey of transformation, helping them build a solid, positive reputation that paves the way for long-term success.

These case studies highlight a positive image's impact on an organization's success. By implementing effective communication and public relations strategies, organizations can craft a positive image that aligns with their values and resonates with their audiences, ultimately driving their success.

Principle 5:
Stay in Your Lane - Fostering Specialization and Collaboration

As the curtains of the twenty-first century continue to unfurl, the dynamics of the organizational world have significantly transformed. The tempo of technological advancements, the globalization of markets, and the complexities of operational processes have necessitated a transition from generalists to specialists within organizations. What does 'stay in your lane' mean within a work environment, and how can we encourage a harmonious balance between specialization and collaboration? This chapter aims to delve into this compelling conundrum.

In an era of knowledge and innovation, clearly understanding roles and specialized functions is paramount. Everyone's expertise, unique skill set, and focus area contribute to the overall success of an organization. Notwithstanding the indispensability of specialization, fostering collaboration and teamwork becomes the cohesive force that synergizes these individual talents towards a shared vision.

However, as organizations strive to be more efficient and cost-effective, professionals are increasingly burdened with multifaceted roles beyond their areas of expertise. This overextension often comes at the cost of peak performance and job satisfaction. The adage "jack of all trades, master of none" succinctly encapsulates this predicament. Moreover, the delusion that one can perform another's job better without comprehending the nuances involved fosters disharmony and undermines the spirit of teamwork.

Drawing parallels from the sports world, consider a football team. A defensive lineman and a quarterback have distinct roles, each honed through specific training and developed skillsets. Just as it would be unproductive to critique the other's methods, it is equally counterproductive for individuals in an organization to overstep their professional boundaries.

In education and healthcare, for instance, the intrusion of non-professionals into areas of expertise often leads to unnecessary contention and distraction. A collaborative effort is undeniably essential, but it should not metamorphose into an overstepping of professional boundaries or unwarranted criticisms.

This chapter will illuminate the importance of specialized roles, elucidate techniques for fostering collaboration, and provide empirical evidence supporting the balance of specialization and teamwork within organizations. We aspire to transform toxic organizational cultures into harmonious, productive, and enriching workspaces by navigating these lanes.

Corporate Example - Software Development Company

The sales and development teams have distinct responsibilities in a mid-sized software development firm. The sales team interfaces with clients, understands their needs, and relays them to the development team. The developers, proficient in coding and software architecture, bring these requirements to life. Consider a situation where a sales representative, despite having little technical knowledge, starts instructing developers on how to code because they believe it might speed up the delivery process. This overstepping results in miscommunications, slowing the development cycle, and subpar product quality due to misguided instructions. Simultaneously, developers' morale takes a hit as they feel undermined by a non-expert.

Recognizing each other's roles and boundaries can go a long way in fostering organizational efficiency. The sales representative should trust the developers' expertise and adhere to their role of accurately conveying the client's needs, allowing the development team to work their magic. Regular meetings can be organized where both teams share updates and concerns and celebrate milestones. These interactions can provide a platform for cross-learning without overstepping boundaries and ensure that each team feels valued, respected, and heard.

Athletics Example - Football Team

In a professional football team, each player has a unique role contributing to the team's success. Imagine a goalkeeper consistently leaving his post to participate in field play, believing he can score better than the strikers. This behavior would leave the goal unprotected and expose the team to unnecessary risks. Furthermore, this could discourage the strikers, causing a dip in their performance and creating a dysfunctional team dynamic.

Every player in a football team brings a unique skill set. Instead of overstepping roles, the goalkeeper can provide feedback or suggestions to the strikers during team meetings and, similarly, learn about the strikers' challenges. Creating a safe space where team members can openly discuss strategies and concerns promotes mutual understanding and cohesion. Moreover, it reinforces the idea that each role, however different, is crucial to the team's overall success.

School Example - High School Environment

In a high school, teachers, administrators, and parents each play a crucial role in a student's education. Suppose some parents, unsatisfied with the curriculum, start dictating teaching methodologies to educators without understanding the pedagogical considerations involved. This can lead to confusion among students, increased stress for teachers, and even potential degradation of educational quality. Moreover, it undermines the professional authority and expertise of the educators, affecting their morale.

Parents and educators want the best for the students, but respecting each party's expertise is crucial. Organizing regular meetings between parents and educators can serve as a platform for parents to voice concerns or suggestions and for teachers to provide insights into pedagogical strategies. This promotes understanding and mutual respect, improving the quality of education and building a stronger school community.

Military Example - Army Unit

In a military unit, every soldier is trained for a specific role, with duties clearly defined by the chain of command. If a logistics officer decides to question the strategy of a combat mission led by a trained and experienced combat officer, it could lead to confusion and dissent and potentially jeopardize the mission's success. It may also cause friction in the ranks, hampering overall unit cohesion and operational effectiveness.

The stakes are high in the military, and trust in each other's skills is paramount. While a logistics officer might have suggestions or concerns regarding a combat mission, these should be raised in an appropriate setting, such as a briefing or debriefing. Understanding and respecting each other's roles can bolster unit cohesion and operational effectiveness. Safe spaces for discussions can enhance mutual respect and enable the unit to function as a coherent, efficient team.

In each case, violating professional boundaries creates friction and confusion and weakens the organization's functionality. The balance between collaboration and respecting expertise is delicate yet paramount to the success of any organizational structure. It is essential that all members, regardless of their position in the hierarchy, recognize and adhere to this principle to facilitate smooth operations and maintain a healthy, productive environment.

It is evident that maintaining professional boundaries, fostering trust, and creating platforms for respectful communication and collaboration can significantly enhance organizational health and productivity. Encouraging individuals to stay in their lanes while providing spaces for dialogue and shared learning ensures that the organization can operate smoothly, scale effectively, and accomplish its objectives.

The Importance of Specialized Roles and Clear Responsibilities within an Organization

Specialization in organizational roles is vital for maintaining efficiency and quality and fostering innovation within an organization. It enables individuals to focus on specific tasks, allowing them to develop expertise and refine their skills, thus enhancing output quality and attention to detail (Burton et al., 2011). As per Ericsson, Krampe, and Tesch-Römer (1993) study, 'deliberate practice' accentuates the significance of task-specific training in developing expert performance.

The benefits of role specialization extend to the customization of training for departmental needs. When roles are delineated, it becomes possible to tailor training programs to cater to the unique needs of each position. Grant (2007) elucidates that this tailored training leads to improved competency, increased job satisfaction, and enhanced performance as employees feel more prepared and competent in their specific roles.

In addition to quality and focus, role specialization also impacts an organization's innovation capabilities. According to Becker and Murphy (1992), as employees specialize and deepen their knowledge in a particular domain, they become more capable of identifying novel solutions and approaches, thereby fostering innovation.

Furthermore, clear responsibilities eliminate ambiguity, leading to an increase in overall organizational efficiency. A study by Stewart and Barrick (2000) confirms that when employees clearly understand their duties, they are more likely to be engaged and productive, leading to improved performance.

However, while specialization is essential, it should be balanced with a degree of cross-functionality to encourage collaboration and avoid a silo mentality (O'Leary, Mortensen, & Woolley, 2011). A clear understanding of roles and responsibilities and effective communication and collaboration ultimately fuels organizational success.

Consider a high-end restaurant with a clear division of specialized roles - chefs, sommeliers, front-of-house staff, managers, etc. Each professional within this setting possesses unique skills and responsibilities crucial for the overall success of the establishment. The chefs are the culinary experts, trained in the art of cooking and presenting dishes. They focus on creating delightful dishes, experimenting with recipes, and maintaining the highest quality standards. Their training is customized according to the cuisine and the dishes they specialize in, whether French cuisine, pastries, or grill.

Sommeliers, on the other hand, are wine experts. Their responsibilities include selecting wines that complement the menu, advising guests, and managing the wine cellar. They undergo specialized training to understand wine varietals, vineyards, and pairing techniques.

The front-of-house staff, including servers and hosts, are trained in customer service, table settings, taking orders, and effectively communicating with the kitchen staff. Their responsibilities are critical in maintaining a positive dining experience for the customers.

The manager oversees overall operations, ensures smooth coordination between roles, handles administrative tasks, and resolves issues.

Each professional's ability to focus on their specialized role, coupled with clear responsibilities, ensures the restaurant operates smoothly and delivers an exceptional dining experience. The chef does not have to worry about wine selection, and the sommelier is not concerned about customer service nuances - each trusts the expertise of their colleagues, leading to increased efficiency and performance. They collaborate, offer suggestions, and learn from each other during team meetings but stay within their roles and duties.

In this environment, both the customers and the professionals benefit - they receive high-quality service, and the professionals can focus on their areas of expertise, continually refine their skills, and take pride in their work.

This example highlights the importance of specialized roles, clear responsibilities, and effective organizational collaboration. It emphasizes how these elements contribute to a higher-quality output and improved efficiency and foster an environment of respect and mutual trust.

Techniques for Promoting Collaboration and Teamwork

While specialization within an organization is integral for efficiency and quality, it must be complemented by collaboration and teamwork to maximize organizational success. Here, we explore empirically validated techniques for fostering organizational partnership and cooperation.

Firstly, fostering a culture of open communication is a cornerstone of collaboration (Levasseur, 2013). Teams that communicate effectively are likelier to share ideas, understand each other's roles, and work together towards common goals. Creating a safe environment where everyone feels comfortable expressing their ideas and concerns without fear of judgment or backlash can significantly enhance collaboration.

Secondly, regular team meetings can promote a shared understanding and build trust among team members (Rogelberg et al., 2007). When properly structured and effectively led, meetings can facilitate problem-solving, decision-making, and coordination, reinforcing the sense of teamwork.

Thirdly, promoting interdependence can strengthen the team's cohesion and collaboration. Thompson (2008) emphasizes the importance of creating team tasks that require mutual reliance among members. This can be achieved through setting team goals or cross-functional projects that necessitate collaboration.

Furthermore, investing in team-building activities can foster teamwork and improve interpersonal relationships among team members (Klein et al., 2009). These activities, ranging from workshops and retreats to more informal social gatherings, can help build trust and understanding, which is crucial for effective collaboration.

Finally, recognizing and rewarding collaboration can incentivize team members to work together (Chen & Kanfer, 2006). When the organization appreciates and rewards collaborative efforts, it encourages team members to share knowledge and support each other.

Research on the Benefits of Specialization and Collaboration in Organizations

The marriage of specialization and collaboration within an organization brings numerous benefits, ranging from increased productivity to heightened innovation. This concept, traced back to Adam Smith's Division of Labor theory, remains pertinent centuries later (Smith, 1776). Contemporary studies consistently uphold Smith's theory, associating specialization with improved efficiency (Becker & Murphy, 1992). Additionally, Wuchty, Jones, and Uzzi's extensive research (2007) established that teams outperform individuals regarding innovation.

Organizations attain optimal adaptability when they balance specialized knowledge and integrated collaboration (Ethiraj & Levinthal, 2004). In the healthcare sector, this balance leads to better patient outcomes, cost savings, and enhanced patient satisfaction (Epstein, 2014). A 2017 report by Deloitte affirms that organizations promoting specialization and collaboration also report less turnover and higher creativity levels.

Promotion and role transitions within an organization serve a unique purpose that should be distinct from specialization. They are instrumental in staving off employee burnout and stagnation, creating a dynamic work environment (Gallup, 2018). Leaders play a pivotal role in these transitions, ensuring that individuals are placed in roles where their skills and attributes can be utilized most effectively (Tulgan, 2016). It is worth emphasizing that promoting role transition and cross-training should not be mistaken for encroaching on professional boundaries. The goal is not to cultivate jacks of all trades but to refine specialization, thereby enhancing productivity (DeFilippo & Arthur, 1994).

Case Study 1: SpaceX

SpaceX, a private American aerospace manufacturer and space transport services company founded by Elon Musk, has often been hailed as a prime example of a specialized, collaborative organization. Each engineer within the company has a specific domain of expertise - propulsion, navigation, or materials science (Vance, 2015). This distinct role division enables employees to excel in their chosen area, reducing the likelihood of errors and improving overall performance.

However, collaboration is the other side of this coin. Teams at SpaceX communicate constantly and openly. They share their successes and failures, creating an atmosphere of mutual learning. As Musk once remarked, "It is imperative to like the people you work with, otherwise life [and] your job is gonna be quite miserable" (Musk, 2017).

The success of this model is evident in SpaceX's ability to disrupt the traditionally government-dominated space industry, offering cheaper and reusable rocket technologies. Employees report a highly collaborative, albeit intense, work environment, fostering an innovative and mission-driven culture.

Case Study 2: Mayo Clinic

Mayo Clinic, one of the leading healthcare organizations in the world, is renowned for its culture of specialized collaboration. They have experts in their fields, but all physicians work together in integrated, multidisciplinary teams for the patient's benefit (Berry & Seltman, 2008).

This unique combination of specialization and collaboration has led to impressive results in patient care. The clinic boasts higher survival rates, fewer complications, and more satisfied patients (Hartzband & Groopman, 2018). Moreover, this approach contributes to a positive work environment, as physicians respect each other's expertise and work together to deliver the best care possible.

In the grand theatre of an organization, each employee plays a crucial role, like actors cast in a carefully crafted script. If one player decides to abandon their part and adopt another's role mid-performance, the harmony of the play shatters. As organizational members, each of us has a unique part to play - a lane where we must stay to ensure the smooth functioning of the organization.

In toxic organizations, where the culture of blame, finger-pointing, and micromanagement has taken root, the 'Staying in Your Lane' principle becomes even more critical. When employees cross lanes and interfere with tasks outside their expertise, it disrupts the symphony of teamwork. The result? Chaos, failure, and a debilitating work culture where much is said but little is done.

Unfortunately, economic necessities and the urge for cross-training often blur these lanes. While training and flexibility are essential, they should not be an excuse for employees to take on roles they are not prepared for regarding skillsets and attitude. We must remember - that an orchestra sounds melodious only when every musician plays their instrument flawlessly, not when the flutist tries their hand at the drums.

Instead, fostering a culture of specialization and collaboration can pave the way for exceptional performance and a nurturing organizational climate. By clearly defining roles and responsibilities, we allow employees to master their craft to own their lane. Simultaneously, encouraging open communication and teamwork enables different lanes to harmonize and create a powerful, coherent narrative.

The beauty of 'Staying in Your Lane' is that it is not about constraining individuals. It is about allowing them to blossom uniquely while contributing to the organization's success. It is about respecting each other's expertise and trusting that everyone is doing their best in their lane.

Imagine an organization where everyone is a master of their domain yet in perfect sync with the team. The quarterback focuses on his throws, trusting that the defensive lineman will hold the line. The doctors diagnose, trusting that the administrative staff will manage the records. In this orchestra, each instrument contributes to the grand symphony, not by playing louder or out of turn, but by playing its part to perfection.

So, let us stay in our lanes, not out of a sense of restriction, but out of respect - for ourselves, our colleagues, and the organization we are all a part of. After all, we are on this journey together. Furthermore, only by acknowledging and respecting our unique roles can we truly unleash the power of collective success.

Principle 6:
Have Fun - Cultivating a Healthy Work Culture

The world of work has undergone a profound transformation. For too many individuals, jobs have often become an unwelcome necessity, a dull routine, and, worst of all, a source of humiliation and anxiety. In some organizations, the atmosphere is so taxing that it borders on harassment, depriving employees of any reward or satisfaction. This harsh reality results from an alarming increase in job vacancies, high turnover rates, a spike in personal or sick leave usage, and a noticeable decrease in productivity. Once a buzzing hub of energy and engagement, the workplace is now a dreary environment that stifles creativity and dampens morale.

The remedy to this bleak scenario may be more straightforward than most leaders think: Fun. Yes, fun. A term that has, in recent years, become the 'new F-word' in organizational discourse, often met with skepticism and even disdain. For many, incorporating fun into the workplace signifies a frivolous, non-serious environment that could hamper productivity and, therefore, should be avoided. However, this misperception is unfounded and contradicts a significant body of empirical research.

Research substantiates that fun at work does not undermine productivity but enhances it. It cultivates a culture that fosters employee morale, job satisfaction, and overall well-being (Tews et al., 2014). When employees are happy, they perform better, are more loyal to their organization, and strongly desire to be part of their community (Boehm & Lyubomirsky, 2008). Moreover, fun-filled, engaging workplaces attract and retain talented employees, reducing turnover and vacancy rates (McDowell, 2004).

What exactly does fun in the workplace entail? Is it office parties and ping-pong tables? Or is it a more profound sense of enjoying one's work, finding it meaningful, and appreciating the relationships formed with colleagues? In the coming chapters, we will explore the concept of fun in the workplace, how it has evolved, and how it can be effectively infused into a company's culture to foster a healthier, more productive, and more satisfying work environment. The key is to strike a balance to create an environment where employees feel that their work is not just a job but also a source of pleasure and fulfillment.

Making the workplace fun is not a passing trend but a fundamental shift in our understanding of what work could and should be. It is imperative for organizations wishing to stay relevant in a rapidly changing business landscape, attract the best talent, and ensure the well-being and productivity of their workforce. In the subsequent sections, we delve deeper into this intriguing topic, demonstrating through empirical evidence, case studies, and practical guidelines that fun is not the adversary of work but its powerful, transformative ally.

In the evolving labor market landscape, a seismic shift in employees' priorities is reshaping the dynamics of the employer-employee relationship. Traditional motivators, primarily salary, are increasingly overshadowed by a new breed of benefits and incentives more aligned with the modern workforce's needs, desires, and lifestyles. The Millennial generation, now a significant portion of the workforce, often willingly trades off higher salaries for various non-monetary benefits that contribute to a more balanced and fulfilling life.

This paradigm shift is primarily driven by the understanding that job satisfaction transcends financial remuneration. Modern workers seek a holistic work environment that nurtures their professional growth, personal well-being, and life satisfaction. As such, organizations are being challenged to think more creatively and expansively about their compensation and benefits packages (Joshi et al., 2011).

Benefits like on-site fitness classes, shorter work weeks, flexible schedules, and the ability to work remotely have become increasingly attractive to many employees. Also popular are perks like extended holidays, personal days for family events, and flexible hours that accommodate employees' varying life demands. Some companies have even gone as far as to offer unique amenities like childcare services, transportation assistance, laundry services, and discounted rates on various products and services (Henneman & Jocz, 2016).

A wealth of research corroborates the efficacy of these non-traditional benefits in enhancing job satisfaction and organizational commitment, leading to lower turnover rates and higher productivity levels (Kossek et al., 2015). Furthermore, providing such benefits can significantly enhance an organization's appeal to potential recruits, serving as a strategic tool for attracting top-tier talent (Casper & Harris, 2008).

The evolving preferences of the modern workforce necessitate a shift in the leadership mindset. To recruit and retain skilled employees, leaders must understand, appreciate, and accommodate their diverse needs and aspirations. They need to shift from a transactional to a transformational approach, where employees' total well-being is valued, and their satisfaction is considered essential for the organization's success.

Examples

Single Mother: Jennifer, a single mother of two young children, recently turned down a higher-paying position at a prestigious firm located an hour's drive away. She instead chose to stay with her current employer, a local company that offered flexible working hours and on-site childcare. This decision allowed her to balance her career with her responsibilities as a mother. Jennifer may have sacrificed a higher salary, but she gained peace of mind and the invaluable ability to be there for her children, enhancing her overall life satisfaction.

College Student: Mark, a full-time college student, declined a high-paying job that would have required him to work rigid hours that interfered with his class schedule. Instead, he accepted a lower-paying position that offered a flexible work schedule and the opportunity to work remotely. Despite the lower pay, Mark's choice facilitated his ability to pursue his education while still earning an income, leading to a balanced and fulfilling student and work life.

Long-Distance Commuter: Sophie, a talented software engineer, was offered an attractive salary package by a renowned tech company. However, accepting the job would have required her to commute over 90 minutes each way. Sophie chose instead to take a position with a slightly lower salary at a company closer to home that offered the ability to work from home several days a week. While her take-home pay was less, Sophie gained more personal time and a higher quality of life by minimizing her commute and work-related stress.

Health-Conscious Employee: James, a highly skilled marketing executive and fitness enthusiast, was offered a lucrative job offer from a large corporation. However, the demanding job would have left little time for his fitness routine. James chose an appointment with a lower salary at a company that provided a state-of-the-art fitness center and encouraged its employees to use it during flexible working hours. James traded a bit of wage for the ability to prioritize his health and well-being, improving his quality of life in the process.

These examples highlight the increasingly prevalent trend among modern workers to prioritize personal well-being, life balance, and overall job satisfaction over salary alone. This shift prompts organizations to rethink compensation and benefits strategies to attract and retain a diverse, talented workforce.

The Significance of a Positive Work Culture in Reducing Toxicity and Promoting Success

Organizational culture significantly influences employee performance, job satisfaction, commitment, and well-being. Positive work culture fosters an environment that promotes fun activities, creativity, diversity, and celebrations and encourages compassion, empathy, and kindness. Research suggests that cultivating such an environment can reduce toxicity and promote organizational success.

The rise of a generation valuing work-life balance and job satisfaction over salary has led to the importance of cultivating a positive work culture. Contemporary employees seek workplaces where they feel valued, appreciated, and free to express their creativity. They want to work in an environment that is not only conducive to professional growth but also personal well-being (Gallup, 2018).

Workplaces that foster enjoyable experiences can lead to greater job satisfaction. Studies by the University of Warwick reveal that happiness can enhance productivity by up to 12%, and employees who enjoy their work exhibit higher motivation and engagement, leading to improved performance (Oswald et al., 2015). Therefore, it is not just an ethical imperative for leaders to promote fun and enjoyment at work but also a practical one.

Moreover, organizations that value diversity and promote inclusivity tend to have a healthier culture. A study conducted by McKinsey & Company indicated that companies with diverse executive teams were 33% more likely to outperform their peers (Hunt et al., 2015). Encouraging diversity in thoughts, ideas, and perspectives fosters innovation and creativity, enhancing problem-solving capabilities and overall business performance.

The significance of compassion, empathy, and kindness in the workplace is also worth noting. These core values lead to improved interpersonal relationships, increased cooperation and collaboration, reduced conflicts, and a supportive work environment (Rynes et al., 2012). The emotional well-being of employees, in turn, impacts their work quality and the organization's overall success.

An organization's culture, which encompasses fun activities, music, food, creativity, diversity, celebrations, professional humor, compassion, empathy, and kindness, can serve as a powerful tool in reducing toxicity and promoting success. It not only boosts employee morale but also enhances productivity and fosters a positive, energetic, infectious atmosphere spreading beyond the office to clients and customers. Therefore, a positive organizational culture is vital for success in today's ever evolving and competitive business environment.

Here are simple, cost-effective ideas to create a more enjoyable work environment that will not pose additional expense or health and safety concerns:

Regular Recognition and Reward Programs: An employee of the month program, shout-outs in meetings for notable achievements, or a simple thank you note can go a long way in making employees feel appreciated and motivated. They can create a culture where employees strive to do their best and help each other to succeed.

Themed Dress-Up Days: Occasional-themed dress-up days (like a favorite sports team day, throwback Thursday, or crazy hat day) can break the routine and add some fun to the workday. These themes should be inclusive and optional to ensure everyone feels comfortable participating.

Breakroom Activities: Providing board games, puzzles, or books in the breakroom can encourage employees to unwind and interact with their colleagues during their breaks, fostering a sense of community.

Learning and Development Sessions: Regular sessions where employees can learn a new skill unrelated to their work can be a great way to foster personal development and break up the work routine. This could include a simple cooking demonstration, a language learning class, or a yoga session.

Collaborative Projects: Encouraging employees from different departments to work together on a project (like a company-wide charity event or internal newsletter) can encourage a sense of unity and teamwork, making the workplace more enjoyable.

Cooking Lessons: Cooking lessons can be a great way to learn new skills and foster team building. It teaches employees to follow instructions, understand the order of operations, and work as a team to create a final product. This could be as simple as making crepes or as exciting as a mocktail-making competition. Plus, it is a fun break from the routine workday.

Comedian Roasts: Inviting a comic to roast the boss or leadership team can be a great way to foster a sense of camaraderie and humor within the workplace. This approach can help humanize the leadership and show that they do not take themselves too seriously, which can improve employee morale and workplace culture.

Motivational Speakers: Hiring a motivational speaker to inspire employees can be a great way to energize the team and introduce fresh perspectives on work and life. It can also boost morale and give employees valuable tools and techniques to manage stress, foster creativity, or improve productivity.

Destination Conferences: Allowing employees to attend training and conferences in popular tourist destinations can make professional development opportunities more enticing. Employees can enhance their skills and knowledge during the day and unwind by exploring the city or attractions in the evening, promoting a better work-life balance.

Leadership Retreats: Organizing leadership retreats or professional development sessions off-site in a resort or recreation area can serve as a refreshing change of scenery. It can foster creativity, strengthen bonds between team members, and boost morale. A relaxed environment might encourage more open, honest discussions and innovative ideas.

Fun Professional Development: Combining professional development with a fun activity, like a morning of learning followed by an afternoon at Top Golf, can make these sessions more engaging and enjoyable. This approach helps balance work and play, keeping employees motivated and excited about their professional growth.

These initiatives aim to balance fun and professionalism, providing employees with a much-needed reprieve from their daily tasks without sacrificing productivity. They promote a positive work culture, strengthen employee bonds, and make the workplace more enjoyable.

Strategies for Encouraging Work-Life Balance and Fostering a Fun Environment

In the 21st century's dynamic work environment, promoting a healthy work-life balance and nurturing an enjoyable workplace is becoming increasingly essential. As workforce demographics and expectations shift, especially among Millennials and Gen Z, organizations are reevaluating their strategies to devise a work culture that is more engaging, flexible, and enjoyable. Implementing these can lead to heightened job satisfaction, improved productivity, and sustained employee retention.

One proven strategy to encourage work-life balance is adopting **flexible work hours** or flexitime (Hill et al., 1996). This allows employees to determine their start and end times for the workday, provided they fulfill their required hours. Research shows that this flexibility can decrease work-family conflict, increase job satisfaction, and promote better physical health (Allen et al., 2013).

Remote or hybrid work models also contribute to a healthier work-life balance. Technological advancements enable many jobs to be performed effectively outside the traditional office, with a study by Bloom et al. (2015) indicating that employees who worked from home reported increased work satisfaction and were notably more productive.

Organizations can introduce **job shadowing opportunities** within and for external visitors to cultivate a fun environment. These could range from children shadowing their parents to potential recruits observing the daily tasks of existing employees. Research suggests that such experiences can boost employee morale and improve the organization's reputation, thus attracting quality talent (Dawson et al., 2011).

Regularly hosting **fun activities** such as karaoke sessions, games, social gatherings, or community services can create a positive work environment. Tews, Michel, & Noe (2017) found that employees who perceive their workplaces as fun exhibit heightened creativity, enhancing job performance.

Providing personal and professional development opportunities such as workshops, seminars, or time off for further education can foster employee engagement and a sense of value (Maurer et al., 2003).

Aesthetic workplace attributes such as clean, organized, bright, and colorful workspaces can significantly impact employee morale and productivity (Dul & Ceylan, 2011). Ensuring well-maintained and stocked breakrooms and restrooms also contributes to a positive and respectful work environment.

Lastly, promoting professionalism and attire that correlates with job duties and functions can instill a sense of pride and commitment to the organization, thereby enhancing morale and productivity (Solomon, 1992).

In implementing these strategies, it is crucial to remember that perceptions of "fun" vary among individuals. Therefore, engaging in discussions with employees to understand their preferences and needs would be beneficial. Organizations can foster a more positive, productive, and satisfying work environment by striking the right balance between work and fun.

Empirical Evidence on the Impact of a Healthy Work Culture on Organizational Performance

A healthy work culture, characterized by job satisfaction, work-life balance, and enjoyable work experiences, is pivotal in driving an organization's performance. The notion of fostering a positive and inclusive work environment, once considered peripheral to strategic management, has now been widely recognized as a crucial determinant of business success. Not only is a healthy work culture instrumental in attracting and retaining talent, but empirical evidence also suggests that it significantly enhances productivity and fosters innovation.

Numerous studies corroborate the relationship between job satisfaction and work performance. For instance, Judge, Thoresen, Bono, and Patton (2001) found a strong positive correlation between job satisfaction and job performance, illustrating that happier employees tend to perform better.

A healthy work culture that prioritizes work-life balance also contributes to better organizational performance. A study by McNall, Nicklin, and Masuda (2010) discovered that a healthy work-life balance increased job satisfaction and reduced stress, consequently enhancing job performance.

Fusing fun into the workplace further strengthens the association between work culture and performance. A study by Tews, Michel, and Bartlett (2012) reported that employees who considered their workplaces fun were more likely to be creative, which improved job performance. Similarly, Karl, Peluchette, and Hall (2008) observed that fun activities in the workplace fostered team cohesion and improved workgroup performance.

Workplaces that promote professional development and continuous learning also improve organizational performance. As suggested by Pajo, Coetzer, and Guenole (2010), employees who perceive their organizations as supportive of their professional growth are more likely to stay, thereby reducing turnover rates and being more engaged in their work.

The impact of workplace aesthetics on performance should be noticed. Vischer (2007) argued that supportive physical work conditions, such as an organized, clean, and colorful environment, positively influence job satisfaction and productivity.

In conclusion, empirical evidence unequivocally supports that a healthy work culture significantly enhances organizational performance. As such, organizations aiming for success should prioritize cultivating a supportive, fun, and fulfilling work environment.

Case Study: AlphaTech Inc. - A Paradigm Shift to an Enjoyable Workplace

AlphaTech Inc., a burgeoning technology company in Silicon Valley, was wrestling with staff retention issues and low productivity levels in 2021. Despite its innovative projects and competitive salaries, employee morale was dwindling, and job satisfaction rates were at an all-time low. Turnover rates were mounting alarmingly, leaving many critical projects at a standstill. Concerned about these issues, AlphaTech's leadership team set out to revamp the company's work culture, transforming the workplace into a more gratifying environment.

Recognizing the mounting evidence suggesting the positive influence of fun at work, AlphaTech embarked on a "Fun at Work" initiative. This encompassed numerous changes to foster an engaging, inclusive, and enjoyable work environment. Fun Fridays were introduced, involving various activities from team-building games and themed dress-up days to cook-offs and karaoke sessions. Spaces within the office were restructured and transformed into creative and collaborative hubs, equipped with comfortable seating, inspirational artwork, and even a game room. Employees were encouraged to use these spaces during breaks for impromptu meetings, brainstorming sessions, or relaxation.

AlphaTech started recognizing and celebrating employee achievements, birthdays, and work anniversaries more visibly to boost morale and cultivate a sense of community. They also introduced a program called "Shadow Days," enabling employees to bring their children or friends to work and showcase their roles and responsibilities.

The company's leadership team also integrated fun into professional development. They hosted workshops and training in off-site locations and arranged for guest speakers from various fields to introduce an element of novelty and excitement. Remote work options allowed employees to balance work and personal life better.

The shift in AlphaTech's work culture, underpinned by the injection of fun into the workplace, led to significant improvements in organizational performance and employee satisfaction. Within a year, the turnover rate dropped by 30%, and the employee satisfaction survey results revealed a 40% improvement. Employees reported feeling more engaged and satisfied, reflected in the 25% increase in productivity.

Moreover, AlphaTech noticed a positive change in its recruitment efforts. The company's fun and flexible work culture attracted more potential candidates, reinforcing AlphaTech's reputation as a desirable workplace. Job vacancies were filled more rapidly, and the quality of new hires improved.

The case of AlphaTech provides compelling evidence of the potential benefits of creating a fun work environment. It serves as a testament to the fact that prioritizing employee enjoyment and satisfaction can significantly improve organizational performance, staff retention, and recruitment. The case illustrates that "fun" is not a detriment to a serious work environment but a powerful tool for cultivating a healthy, productive, and appealing work culture.

In a rapidly evolving work environment, understanding the power of cultivating a fun, healthy, and satisfying workplace becomes a critical success factor for organizations. This chapter underscored the importance of transforming traditional work structures, infusing vibrancy and enjoyment into the work atmosphere to alleviate job-related stress and burnout, thereby enhancing productivity and performance. It highlighted the value of rethinking compensation strategies, underscoring the increasing preference of today's workforce for enhanced benefits and flexibility over mere monetary gains. We delved into the significance of a positive work culture, showing how team-building events, professional humor, and celebrating achievements can enhance camaraderie, promote collaboration, and, ultimately, drive organizational success. We also explored strategies to foster a balance between work and life, including remote work, job shadowing, and maintaining a conducive work environment. These principles were illustrated vividly through the case study of AlphaTech Inc., where introducing a fun, flexible work environment led to remarkable improvements in turnover rates, job satisfaction, and productivity. Conclusively, creating an enjoyable work atmosphere is a desirable ideal and a strategic imperative for organizations aiming for sustainable success in today's dynamic landscape.

Principle 7:
Influence - Leveraging Leadership for Lasting Change

In this chapter, we will delve into the heart of organizational change, the seventh and arguably most impactful principle of our journey: Influence - Leveraging Leadership for Lasting Change. The essence of this principle lies in its resonance with the science of system dynamics, revealing that organizations are akin to intricate networks of interconnected components, each influencing and being influenced by others (Sterman, 2000).

Organizations are complex entities, vast ecosystems where change ripples across every corner, no matter how minor the originating action might seem. Many organizational leaders need to understand this complexity as a call to address every emerging issue simultaneously, often leading to the dispersal of resources, overwhelming effort, and little sustainable progress. This scattergun approach can be a perilous pitfall, leading organizations into cycles of 'firefighting' and 'band-aid' solutions, resulting in little genuine, lasting change (Senge, 2006).

Successful organizations, on the other hand, have mastered a more refined, strategic approach. They embrace the complexities of their environments, identifying two or three key leverage points that, when addressed, will ripple throughout the organization, influencing numerous other areas (Meadows, 1999). Focusing on these pivotal points, they harness the interconnectedness inherent in their structure to maximize their influence, minimize their efforts, and optimize their results.

Similarly, in the human landscape of organizations, individuals who are, by nature or design, more influential than others. These individuals can precipitate significant shifts in attitude, culture, and performance within the organization (Cialdini, 2001). Rather than trying to motivate everyone independently, savvy leaders recognize these influencers and empower them, harnessing their natural abilities to stimulate, persuade, and inspire others. Incorporating these influencers into their leadership teams strengthens their leadership cadre and extends their reach and impact throughout the organization.

This chapter explores the power of the principle of influence in the realm of leadership and organizational change. We will examine strategies to identify critical organizational leverage points and influencers and discuss how these can be harnessed to drive effective, lasting change.

Let us now delve into influence dynamics, unravel its intricacies, and discover how it can be the lynchpin in our journey towards lasting organizational change."

Consider the example of a large multinational technology company, which we will call 'TechGlobal.' TechGlobal faced declining employee morale, decreased productivity, and increasing turnover rates. The company's leadership initially attempted to tackle these problems independently, setting up separate task forces for each one. However, the situation continued to worsen.

Taking a step back, TechGlobal's leadership decided to employ a system dynamics perspective. They undertook an in-depth analysis and discovered two key leverage points: the quality of mid-level management and the company's performance review process. Both were identified as having a significant influence on their major challenges.

TechGlobal decided to concentrate its efforts on these two areas. They implemented a comprehensive training program to enhance the skills of their mid-level managers and revamped their performance review process to be more transparent and constructive. These changes had a ripple effect throughout the organization. Improved management practices led to a boost in employee morale, subsequently increasing productivity. Furthermore, the revamped performance review process made employees feel more valued, reducing turnover.

Within this example, the key influencers were the mid-level managers who could use their leadership roles to positively influence their respective teams after receiving the necessary training. TechGlobal catalyzed meaningful, sustainable organizational change by focusing on these influential individuals and critical processes.

This exemplifies the power of identifying and focusing on an organization's leverage points and key influencers. It highlights the potential for a few well-placed actions to create extensive and impactful changes, embodying the essence of Principle 7: Influence - Leveraging Leadership for Lasting Change.

The Role of Effective Leadership in Driving Organizational Transformation

Organizations exist in a complex web of interdependencies, a principle embodied in system dynamics. Every part of an organization is intrinsically linked to others, and actions in one area invariably impact others. This complex web of interactions shapes the system's behavior, emphasizing the need for an effective leadership model to navigate this intricacy (Senge, 1990).

Leaders are positioned at the nexus of these interconnected elements, possessing the potential to trigger substantial change across the organization. Applying systems thinking—a holistic approach to analysis that focuses on how a system's parts interrelate—they can pinpoint the most influential elements within their systems. These are the elements that, when acted upon, generate the most significant cascading effects throughout the system (Skarzauskiene, 2010).

Successful leaders move beyond old mental models and special interests, which can often obscure decision-making processes with bias. Instead, they rely on data and organic observations, resisting the pull of previous practices that might steer them away from uncovering the authentic vital influencers within their systems. This departure from bias allows for evidence-based decision-making, steering the organization toward meaningful transformation.

Applying the Pareto Principle, or the 80-20 rule, exemplifies this concept. This principle, introduced by Italian economist Vilfredo Pareto, posits that approximately 80% of effects come from 20% of causes (Koch, 2011). Concentrating on the top 20% of influential issues for leaders and organizational change will produce about 80% of the desired outcomes.

Identifying the influential '20%' is not simply a matter of data analysis; it demands discernment of what is most influential and logistically feasible. Applying the Pareto Principle alongside John Kotter's Change Leadership Model—which underscores creating a climate for change, engaging and enabling the whole organization, and implementing and sustaining change—can be instrumental in navigating this process (Kotter, 1996).

Effective leadership is not just about wielding power or authority. It revolves around understanding the dynamics of the organizational system and identifying where to apply effort for maximum impact. Leaders leverage the power of influence to instigate and sustain lasting change.

Here is a practical illustration to demonstrate this concept:

Consider a highly successful software development company. The CEO, Alex, is well-known within the industry for her innovative approach to leadership. Alex adheres to a different mantra, unlike many leaders who may often be ensnared in day-to-day tasks such as paperwork, phone calls, and countless meetings. She believes in the power of visibility and the strength of organic understanding.

Each day, Alex sets aside time to leave her office and walk around the organization. She visits different departments, observes the workflows, engages in conversations with employees, and actively seeks to understand the undercurrents of the work environment. She does not just wish to know the what of their work but the how and why. This builds a unique level of credibility for Alex as a leader. Her presence is a constant reminder of her engagement and commitment to understanding her organization's needs and intricacies.

However, Alex still needs to pay attention to her administrative duties. Instead, she has empowered her leadership team by delegating many tasks. By identifying and nurturing the abilities of her deputies, she has created a system where administrative tasks are handled efficiently, and she can dedicate her time to observing, listening, and providing feedback.

In practice, Alex might discover that one team seems more stressed than others. Upon closer observation, she realizes they need help with a new software tool that was recently implemented. Rather than dismissing their struggle or dictating a solution from her office, she engages with the team, seeks to understand the challenges, and involves them in finding a solution. She may also realize that this issue could surface in other departments and take proactive measures to address it.

This is an instance where Alex has identified a significant '20%' - the influential issue causing unnecessary stress and reduced productivity. By addressing this issue, Alex influences an '80%' outcome, fostering a more positive work environment and enhancing organizational productivity. Her engagement and approach align with Kotter's Change Leadership Model, as she creates a climate for change and engages the whole organization in the process (Kotter, 1996).

Alex modeled effective leadership and transcended the notion of a leader confined to their office. It is about creating a dynamic, interconnected system where leaders are visible, engaged, and deeply aware of the gears that drive their organizations.

Techniques for developing influential leaders and cultivating leadership skills.

Effective leadership is a central force behind any thriving organization. It is about empowering, inspiring, and leveraging the capabilities of each team member to bring about transformative change. However, as with any aspect of an organization's life, there exist disparities among its people concerning their desire to grow, learn, and lead, as well as their personality traits and work ethic.

Let us divide the workforce into two broad categories: 'high-potentials' who are motivated, engaged, and willing to learn and grow, and 'low-potentials' who exhibit reluctance, insubordination, or a lack of desire to advance. The goal is to develop leadership skills, but the approaches may vary.

For high-potentials, the strategy is relatively straightforward: Empowerment. Create opportunities for them to lead, give them access to professional development resources, and provide regular, constructive feedback. Encourage a culture of mentorship where seasoned leaders guide these emerging ones. This could involve job rotations, shadowing, or even formalized leadership programs. Foster an environment that allows them to take risks, learn from failures, and continuously improve (Day, 2001).

Here are some critical strategies for developing, and cultivating influential leaders:

1. **Mentorship Programs**: Encourage experienced leaders to mentor high-potential employees. This can provide them with firsthand insights and experiences about organizational leadership.

2. **Training and Development Opportunities**: Offer workshops, seminars, or online courses on developing leadership skills. This can range from negotiation skills to decision-making and strategic planning.

3. **Job Rotation or Shadowing**: Give employees a chance to take on different organizational roles or shadow a leader. This exposure can help them understand various aspects of the organization, develop a broader perspective, and build empathy for different roles.

4. **Regular Feedback and Constructive Criticism**: Provide consistent feedback on their performance. This includes praising their achievements, giving constructive feedback on areas of improvement, and guiding them toward their career goals.

5. **Create a Safe Environment for Risk-Taking**: Allow emerging leaders to take calculated risks. This provides them the opportunity to learn from both successes and failures.

6. **Transparent Growth Opportunities**: Clearly communicate the organization's growth and promotion path. This transparency can inspire employees to strive for leadership positions.

7. **Promote Collaborative Work Culture**: Foster a culture that values teamwork, open communication, and mutual respect. This can help future leaders develop vital interpersonal skills.

8. **Recognition and Reward**: Acknowledge and reward employees' personal development efforts and contribute to the organization's success. This can significantly enhance their motivation and engagement.

9. **Addressing Toxic Behavior**: Ensure unacceptable behaviors are not tolerated and handled appropriately. This sets the right expectations for all employees and helps maintain a healthy work environment.

10. **Self-development**: Encourage future leaders to take responsibility for their growth. This includes reading leadership books, attending networking events, and seeking external mentorship.

Remember, these strategies are not one-size-fits-all. They must be tailored to each individual's needs, capabilities, and goals.

Simultaneously, it is essential to address the low potential. Understand that an unwillingness to grow or change may stem from various sources, such as insecurity, lack of knowledge, or the fear of failure. Strive to create an environment that addresses these concerns. Provide training, improve transparency about growth opportunities, and encourage open communication. Recognize and reward positive changes, no matter how small. However, if all efforts fail, leaders must be ready to make tough decisions for the betterment of the organization, even if it involves departmental changes or termination.

Here are a few strategies to manage low-potential employees effectively:

1. **Clear Communication**: Express your concerns about their performance or attitude. Discuss their potential and the benefits of adopting a more constructive approach.

2. **Performance Improvement Plans**: If there are apparent issues with their performance, create a plan outlining the changes that need to be made, with clear metrics and a timeline.

3. **Provide Training and Support**: Offer additional training or support to help them improve. Some people struggle due to a lack of skills or understanding rather than a lack of motivation.

4. **Counseling and Coaching**: Professional counseling or coaching may be beneficial if the issue lies more with attitude or personal issues.

5. **Reassignment**: If an individual is not a fit for their current role, consider whether they might be more successful in a different role within the organization.

6. **Termination**: If all else fails and the individual is negatively impacting the organization, it may be necessary to terminate their employment. This decision must be made fairly, transparently, and in line with HR practices.

7. **Limit Time Investment**: Lastly, remember the Pareto principle. Focus your time and resources on individuals likely to yield the best results for the organization. Sometimes, cultivating high-potential individuals is more beneficial than spending too much time trying to change those who resist improvement.

Managing low-potential individuals involves a balance between offering opportunities for improvement and making the tough decision to part ways when necessary. Always ensure you have given them a chance to grow and improve before considering more drastic measures.

Indeed, as Todd Whitaker eloquently puts it, "The culture of any organization is shaped by the worst behavior the leader is willing to tolerate" (Whitaker, 2012). Leaders, thus, cannot afford to ignore toxic behaviors in the hope that others will too. This adversely affects the morale and productivity of the entire organization.

To illustrate, imagine a team with an exceptionally talented but notably insubordinate member. The leader might fear losing the talent and, therefore, tolerate the insubordination. However, this tolerance undermines the leader's authority and demotivates the rest of the team. It sends a message that such behavior is acceptable, further deteriorating the team dynamics.

In contrast, if necessary, an effective leader would address this issue head-on through counseling, disciplinary actions, or termination. This approach signals to the rest of the team that while talent is valuable, it does not warrant toxicity, uplifting the team's morale and reinforcing a positive work culture.

Developing influential leaders and cultivating leadership skills require a multi-faceted approach. It involves empowering those eager to lead, striving to motivate the unwilling, and having the courage to make tough decisions when necessary.

Consider the case of a rapidly expanding digital marketing agency. Amid growth, they hired Martin, a senior graphic designer whose performance and attitude negatively affected the team dynamics. Initially, the leadership team tried clear communication, where they had a direct conversation with Martin about his role, his impact on the team's morale, and the company's expectations of him. Martin was also allowed to voice out any issues he might be facing.

Despite this, Martin's behavior and performance did not improve, leading to the initiation of a Performance Improvement Plan (PIP). This plan detailed measurable goals for Martin to achieve within a set timeframe. However, even with the PIP, there was no significant change in Martin's performance or attitude.

Next, the leadership team offered Martin additional training and professional development opportunities to help improve his skills and attitude. However, even these measures did not result in the desired changes. The team then considered reassignment. Martin was moved to a different department that might better align with his skills and interests, but his unwillingness to adopt the team culture persisted.

Finally, after exhausting all options, the leadership team terminated Martin's employment. This was done transparently, following all HR protocols.

Following this experience, the leadership team understood the importance of investing time and resources in cultivating high-potential employees. They continued their efforts to help all employees grow, but they also recognized the value of focusing on the 20% of the team that could yield 80% of the results.

Case Studies on the Impact of Strong Leadership in Transforming Toxic Organizations

Microsoft
The annals of business are rife with examples of strong, influential leadership transforming organizations from toxicity and inefficiency into thriving, profitable entities. For this section, we will highlight one such case - the transformation of Microsoft under the leadership of its CEO, Satya Nadella.

Satya Nadella took the reins of Microsoft in 2014 when the company was beset with many problems. The organization was considered toxic, with intense internal competition and employee dissatisfaction. Microsoft's stock prices were stagnant, and its products needed to match the competition from Apple and Google.

The situation needed a strong, decisive, and influential leader to turn things around - and Nadella rose to the occasion.

One of Nadella's first initiatives was to change Microsoft's vision from a "devices and services" company to a "productivity and platform" company. This new vision focused on developing software and services that increase productivity in businesses and individuals, and it required a shift from intense competition to collaboration within the company (Nadella, S. (2017).

To drive this transformation, Nadella identified vital issues to address. He tackled the issue of a toxic work environment by promoting a culture of learning over a culture of know-it-all. He emphasized empathy, diversity, and inclusion - building a safe and accepting culture where employees feel valued and appreciated.

Regarding Pareto's Principle, Nadella identified key areas like Cloud Computing and AI where Microsoft could gain a competitive edge. Significant resources were allocated towards these fields, leading to the development of successful products like Azure and improvements in AI capabilities.

Under Nadella's leadership, Microsoft's revenues increased significantly. The company's stock price has quadrupled since Nadella took over, and employee satisfaction ratings have drastically increased. In 2020, Microsoft was named the most attractive employer in the world by Universum, a clear testament to the transformative power of effective, influential leadership (Universum, 2020).

Starling Elementary School
A profound example of leadership transforming a struggling educational institution can be found in the story of Starling Elementary School, located in an urban district in the United States. Before 2010, the school was marred by high student absenteeism, declining enrollment, low staff morale, and subpar student achievement. It was a classic case of an educational institution spiraling into a cycle of negativity and underperformance.

The transformation of Starling Elementary School started with the appointment of a new principal, Dr. Miranda Rodriguez, in the fall of 2010. Dr. Rodriguez recognized that the failing school needed a radical change in its leadership approach to address its issues.

She identified a small set of critical areas where change could significantly influence the entire school system, effectively applying Pareto's Principle. She identified priority issues: improving student attendance, fostering a positive school culture, and strengthening staff capacity.

To improve student attendance, Dr. Rodriguez started with an initiative to call the parents of each absent student every day personally. This created a sense of accountability and commitment among the parents, immediately improving student attendance.

Dr. Rodriguez implemented a school-wide program promoting kindness, respect, and teamwork to foster a positive school culture. She introduced daily school-wide morning meetings where positive behavior was celebrated, fostering a sense of community and belonging.

Dr. Rodriguez implemented a comprehensive professional development program focusing on effective teaching strategies and collaborative planning to strengthen staff capacity. She also recognized the importance of addressing the staff morale issue. She introduced regular staff recognition and celebration events and provided constructive feedback, making teachers feel valued and appreciated.

Dr. Rodriguez's focused, strategic leadership profoundly affected Starling Elementary School. Student attendance improved drastically, and enrollment grew steeply with the improved school climate and culture. Teachers felt more valued and motivated, leading to a significant improvement in staff retention. This turnaround in the school environment eventually reflected in the student's academic performance, which improved exponentially over the next few years.

This case study is a testament to the power of focused, strategic leadership in turning around a struggling institution. It underscores the importance of strategically identifying key issues, allocating resources, and fostering a positive and inclusive environment to drive improvement and success.

Influencing Change Through Focused Leadership

In this fast-paced, interconnected world, organizational success increasingly depends on embracing change, addressing complexity, and innovation. Organizations are intricate systems with many moving parts, with many concerns vying for attention, effort, and resources. As leaders, we often fall into the trap of becoming 'jacks of all trades, masters of none' — attempting to address all issues simultaneously, thereby diluting our efforts and minimizing our impact.

The overarching concept of Principle 7: Influence – Leveraging Leadership for Lasting Change, is honing our attention on a select few areas of influence. Our focus should not be scattered over all issues but instead sharply directed at those vital few that drive an immense impact. By identifying these key influence areas, leaders can allocate resources efficiently and effect significant and lasting change throughout the organization.

Throughout this chapter, we have delved into the importance of this focus, using the principles of systems dynamics and change leadership to elucidate the concept. We saw that a leader's role is not to control every variable but to discern the most influential elements and devote attention to those. This way, their efforts ripple across the system, creating change far beyond their immediate scope.

As leaders, we must remember that our organizations are more than a collection of processes and outcomes. They are a group of individuals, each with unique motivations, abilities, and potential. We saw the importance of developing a cadre of influential leaders within the organization and equipping them with the tools and opportunities they need to thrive. However, the ability to identify those who resist change and to handle these individuals strategically to prevent their negativity from infiltrating the organization is equally essential.

As we close this chapter, we return to the case studies of Microsoft and Starling Elementary School, two striking examples of the transformative power of focused leadership. These stories remind us that no organization is beyond redemption, and no challenge is too great to overcome. They demonstrate the profound changes that can be affected when leaders courageously choose to influence, change, and lead.

When leaders employ this focused, practical approach, they create tangible improvements in performance outcomes, productivity, and profits and catalyze positivity and growth. A culture that encourages engagement, innovation, and joy. A place where stakeholders find not only success but peace of mind.

As we go forward, let us remember that our goal is not to fix everything at once but to concentrate our efforts where we can make the most difference. Furthermore, in doing so, we become masters of influence, leaders who leave a legacy of change.

Conclusion: Sustaining the Flame – Maintaining Success through the BonFire Principles

The vitality and success of an organization depend on its ability to grow, adapt, and evolve. Whether a fledgling startup, a venerable institution, a struggling business, or a thriving corporation, organizations must stay energized in the rapidly changing landscape of the 21st century. However, the path to transformative change often has obstacles, pitfalls, and formidable challenges. From addressing toxic organizational dynamics to fostering a culture of growth and collaboration, leaders must navigate a complex web of issues to effect lasting change.

This final chapter of our journey draws together the threads of the previous sections to weave a coherent and compelling vision for sustainable organizational success. We revisit the BonFire Principles, each a beacon illuminating a critical facet of successful organizational transformation. These principles represent the culmination of extensive empirical research and experiential knowledge and embody lessons drawn from diverse sectors, industries, and organizational types.

In this chapter, we journey from the ashes of dysfunction to the zenith of excellence, illuminating the transformative power of the BonFire Principles. Each principle is revisited, underscoring its importance, demonstrating its effectiveness through case studies, and offering practical strategies for implementation. Together, these principles form a comprehensive roadmap for organizations seeking to rise from the ashes of mediocrity or dysfunction to achieve and sustain the flame of success.

As we explore each principle, remember that the journey to success is not solitary. It demands collective action, shared commitment, and unwavering determination from all stakeholders. Embrace the transformative power of the BonFire Principles and set your organization on a course for enduring success, from ashes to excellence.

Illuminating the path to sustainable success through the powerful lens of the BonFire Principles. Welcome to the concluding chapter: 'Sustaining the Flame - Maintaining Success through the BonFire Principles.'

The BonFire Principles, forged from empirical research and experience, provide a robust framework for effective organizational transformation. Each principle focuses on a critical aspect of organizational success, spotlighting potential pitfalls and illuminating a path forward. Let us revisit these principles and explore their broad applicability across various sectors and contexts.

Principle 1: Keep it Vanilla - Simplifying Systems for Success
This principle emphasizes the power of simplicity and clarity in organizational systems. Whether in a high-tech startup aiming to streamline its product development process or a healthcare provider seeking to enhance the patient experience, simplifying systems fosters efficiency, reduces confusion, and supports an organization's core mission.

Principle 2: Do not Feed Monsters - Addressing Dysfunctional Dynamics
Toxic behaviors and individuals can stifle growth and breed discontent in any organization. This principle guides leaders in sectors ranging from education to manufacturing in identifying and addressing destructive patterns, fostering a healthier and more productive environment.

Principle 3: Water Flowers, Not Weeds - Nurturing Talent and Growth
Recognizing and nurturing potential is crucial across all sectors. This principle guides leaders in fostering a growth mindset, encouraging professional development in an academic institution, or promoting innovative thinking in a tech enterprise.

Principle 4: You are PR - Crafting a Positive Organizational Image

A positive public image is an asset for any organization. This principle underscores the importance of effective communication and PR strategies for non-profit organizations enhancing their outreach efforts or corporations managing their brand image.

Principle 5: Stay in Your Lane - Fostering Specialization and Collaboration

Specialization and collaboration are critical drivers of organizational success. This principle aids leaders in industries as diverse as finance and hospitality, promoting teamwork and clarity of roles and responsibilities.

Principle 6: Have Fun - Cultivating a Healthy Work Culture

A positive work culture can invigorate an organization, fostering employee satisfaction and boosting performance. This principle is relevant across sectors, from tech companies promoting work-life balance to schools cultivating a positive learning environment.

Principle 7: Influence - Leveraging Leadership for Lasting Change

The power of effective leadership is universally recognized. This principle is integral to sectors across the board, helping leaders leverage their influence for transformative change in governmental organizations or retail enterprises.

While distinctly defined, these principles work in synergy to fuel the transformative journey of an organization. Across sectors, organizations, and contexts, the BonFire Principles offer a universally applicable and empirically sound framework for lasting success.

Strategies for Ongoing Improvement and Maintaining Long-Term Success

Success in transforming an organization is not a singular event but a continuous journey. To maintain long-term success, leaders must embrace a mindset of perpetual growth and improvement. Here are some strategies grounded in the BonFire Principles to aid in this endeavor:

1. Regularly Review Systems: No system is perfect; even the best can become outdated or ineffective. Regularly reviewing organizational systems, as suggested by Principle 1, allows for the identification and rectification of inefficiencies. This iterative process of evaluation and refinement enables an organization to adapt and evolve in an ever-changing environment.

2. Foster Open Communication: Principle 2 underlines the importance of addressing dysfunctional dynamics. One way to ensure this is through fostering open communication. Regularly checking in with your team and encouraging open feedback helps to identify potential issues early on and address them before they develop into significant problems.

3. Cultivate a Culture of Learning: As outlined in Principle 3, nurturing talent is crucial. Cultivating a culture of continuous learning and development aids in keeping your team's skills fresh and up-to-date. Regular training sessions, workshops, and professional development opportunities help foster this growth culture.

4. Maintain Brand Integrity: According to Principle 4, crafting a positive image is vital. Consistently upholding your brand's values in all internal and external interactions is crucial to maintaining this image. Your brand should reflect your organizational culture and values consistently.

5. Promote Collaboration: Encouraging a culture of collaboration, as espoused by Principle 5, helps maintain a sense of unity and purpose. Regular team-building activities and collaborative projects can foster a sense of belonging and improve team dynamics.

6. Celebrate Success: Principle 6 underlines the importance of a healthy work culture. Celebrating successes, big and small, contributes to a positive work environment. Regularly acknowledging and appreciating your team's hard work helps to maintain high levels of motivation and job satisfaction.

7. Continually Develop Leadership: As per Principle 7, leveraging leadership is vital. Regular leadership training and development help to ensure that leadership skills remain sharp and effective. Furthermore, developing future leaders within the organization ensures continuity and stability.

By continually applying and adapting these strategies, leaders can help their organizations thrive, ensuring their transformation is not a flash in the pan but a long-lasting flame of success. Remember, in the journey of organizational transformation, there is no finish line—only new milestones to achieve and new heights to reach.

Hope on the Horizon: The Promising Future with the BonFire Principles

As we draw this journey to a close, we extend a heartfelt acknowledgment to you, the leaders who have embarked on organizational transformation. We recognize your resilience and dedication, the countless hours spent trying to cultivate positive change in a system that often feels resistant. We understand the sleepless nights, the balance between work and life teetering precariously, and the sacrifices you have made to pursue a vision only you seem to see.

In such times, when the path forward is blurred, remember this: the BonFire Principles are not just strategies for organizational change - they are an ethos for a fulfilling, balanced life.

When you apply these principles to your organization, you are not just transforming a system. You are creating an environment that values its people, respects their time, acknowledges their hard work, and promotes their well-being. By fostering such a culture, you boost organizational success and breathe life into your world. The benefits seep beyond work boundaries, enriching all aspects of life, from family to health, recreation to personal peace.

Too many leaders are brought into organizations floundering in the depths of dysfunction and despair, expected to conjure miracles somehow. However, with the BonFire Principles, you are not a solitary magician but a harmonious orchestra conductor directing a triumphant symphony. By instilling these principles, you transform the disarray into harmony, turning the individual notes into a resonating symphony of success.

Applying these principles offers you more than just improved performance metrics. It promises the gift of time - time to spend with your family, time for self-care, and time for leisure. It offers the prospect of a healthy organizational climate that positively impacts every stakeholder's mental and emotional well-being.

The road may be extended and daunting, but the BonFire Principles are the beacon of hope illuminating the path. They provide a framework that does not just make organizational success possible but is also sustainable. Remember, the fire that burns the brightest is not ignited by a spark; it is cultivated with patience, perseverance, and principle. Furthermore, once lit, it can set your organization ablaze with success.

So, as you continue your journey, remember that hope is on the horizon. Transformation is not just within your reach but within your control. With the BonFire Principles, you are not just igniting change but fueling an enduring flame. You are the architect of your success and the success of your organization. Rise from the ashes, soar to the heights of excellence, and watch your organization radiate with the iridescent glow of the BonFire Principles. Believe in the process, trust the journey, and success will become an aspiration and an inevitability.

APPENDIX: EMPIRICAL EVIDENCE, CASE STUDIES, AND METHODOLOGIES

Aaker, D. A. (2012). Building strong brands. Simon and Schuster.

Allen, T. D., Johnson, R. C., Kiburz, K. M., & Shockley, K. M. (2013). Work–family conflict and flexible work arrangements: Deconstructing flexibility. *Personnel Psychology*, *66*(2), 345–376.

Amabile, T., & Kramer, S. (2011). The progress principle: Using small wins to ignite joy, engagement, and creativity at work. Harvard Business Press.

Bacal, R. (2016). Toxic organizations and people: The autonomous antidote for toxic behavior. Industrial and Commercial Training, 48(3), 118-122. https://doi.org/10.1108/ICT-08-2015-0055

Barker, R. (2008). Effective organizational communication: Perspectives, principles, and practices. Pearson Education.

Barsade, S. G., & O'Neill, R. M. (2014). What's love got to do with it? A longitudinal study of the culture of companionate love and employee and client outcomes in a long-term care setting. Administrative Science Quarterly, 59(4), 551–598.

Becker, G. S., & Murphy, K. M. (1992). The Division of Labor, Coordination Costs, and Knowledge. *Quarterly Journal of Economics*, *107*(4), 1137–1160.

Bennis, W. (2009). On becoming a leader. Basic Books.

Berry, L. L., & Seltman, K. D. (2008). Management Lessons from Mayo Clinic: Inside One of the World's Most Admired Service Organizations. McGraw Hill Professional.

Bloom, N., Liang, J., Roberts, J., & Ying, Z. J. (2015). Does working from home work? Evidence from a Chinese experiment. *The Quarterly Journal of Economics, 130*(1), 165–218.

Boehm, J. K., & Lyubomirsky, S. (2008). Does happiness promote career success? Journal of Career Assessment, 16(1), 101-116

Bonn, C. (2023). The best way to kill a monster is to stop feeding it! BonFire Leadership Solutions LLC.

Burton, R. M., Obel, B., & DeSanctis, G. (2011). Organizational design: A step-by-step approach (2nd ed.). Cambridge University Press.

Cable, D. M., & Turban, D. B. (2003). The value of organizational reputation in the recruitment context: A brand-equity perspective. Journal of Applied Social Psychology, 33(11), 2244–2266.

Cialdini, R. B. (2001). Influence: Science and practice (4th ed.). Allyn & Bacon.

Cerasoli, C. P., Nicklin, J. M., & Ford, M. T. (2014). Intrinsic motivation and extrinsic incentives jointly predict performance: A 40-year meta-analysis. Psychological Bulletin, 140(4), 980-1008. doi:10.1037/a0035661

Chen, G., & Kanfer, R. (2006). Toward a systems theory of motivated behavior in work teams. Research in Organizational Behavior, 27, 223-267.

Cohen, S. G., & Blake, R. S. (2016). Confronting the toxic employee. Organizational Dynamics, 45(1), 65-74. https://doi.org/10.1016/j.orgdyn.2016.02.003

Collins, J. (2001). Good to great: Why some companies leap...and others don't. Harper Business.

Coombs, W. T. (2007). Protecting organization reputations during a crisis: The development and application of situational crisis communication theory. Corporate reputation review, 10(3), 163–176.

Copeland, R. (2018). Microsoft's Nadella talks about company's 'long journey' back. Wall Street Journal. Retrieved from https://www.wsj.com/articles/microsofts-nadella-talks-about-companys-long-journey-back-1540309201

Covey, S. R. (2021). The 7 habits of highly effective people: Powerful lessons in personal change. Free Press.

Covey, S. R. (1989). The 7 Habits of highly effective people. Simon & Schuster.

Darling-Hammond, L. (2000). Teacher quality and student achievement: A review of state policy evidence. Education Policy Analysis Archives, 8(1), 1–44.

Dawson, M., Abbott, J., & Shoemaker, S. (2011). The Hospitality Culture Scale: A measure organizational culture and personal attributes. *International Journal of Hospitality Management, 30*(2), 290–300.

Day, D. V. (2001). Leadership development: A review in context. Leadership Quarterly, 11(4), 581-613.

DeFilippo, D. N., & Arthur, W. B. (1994). Employee fit and job satisfaction in a job design context. *Journal of Business and Psychology, 8*(4), 445–459.

Deephouse, D. L. (2000). Media reputation as a strategic resource: Integrating mass communication and resource-based theories. Journal of Management, 26(6), 1091–1112.

Deloitte (2017). 2017 Global Human Capital Trends. Deloitte University Press.

Dorn, M., & Dorn, S. (2014). Staying alive: How to act fast and survive deadly encounters. Barron's Educational Series.

Druker, P. F. (2008). The essential Drucker: The best sixty years of Peter Drucker's essential writings on management. Harper Collins

DuFour, R., DuFour, R., Eaker, R., & Many, T. (2010). Learning by doing: A handbook for professional learning communities at work. Solution Tree Press.

Dul, J., & Ceylan, C. (2011). Work environments for employee creativity. Ergonomics, 54(1), 12-20.

Durlak, J. A., Weissberg, R. P., Dymnicki, A. B., Taylor, R. D., & Schellinger, K. B. (2011). The impact of enhancing students' social and emotional learning: A meta-analysis of school-based universal interventions. Child Development, 82(1), 405-432.

Dweck, C. S. (2006). *Mindset: The new psychology of success.* Random House

Einarsen, S., Skogstad, A., Rørvik, E., Lande, Å. B., & Nielsen, M. B. (2016). Climate for conflict management, exposure to workplace bullying and work engagement: A moderated mediation analysis. The International Journal of Human Resource Management, 27(22), 2723-2742. https://doi.org/10.1080/09585192.2015.1091368

Epstein, A. M. (2014). Revisiting Readmissions—Changing the Incentives for Shared Accountability. *The New England Journal of Medicine, 376*(16), 499–501.

Ericsson, K. A., Krampe, R. T., & Tesch-Römer, C. (1993). The role of deliberate practice in the acquisition of expert performance. Psychological Review, 100(3), 363–406

Ethiraj, S. K., & Levinthal, D. (2004). Bounded Rationality and the Search for Organizational Architecture: An Evolutionary

Perspective on the Design of Organizations and Their Evolvability. *Administrative Science Quarterly, 49*(3), 404–437.

Fisher, D., Frey, N., & Pumpian, I. (2012). How to create a culture of achievement in your school and classroom. ASCD.

Fullan, M. (2020). Leading in a culture of change. John Wiley & Sons.

Fullan, M. (2001). Leading in a culture of change. Jossey-Bass.

Gallup (2018). State of the American Workplace. Gallup, Inc.

Grant, A. M. (2007). Relational job design and the motivation to make a prosocial difference. *Academy of Management Review, 32*(2), 393–417.

Grant, H., & Dweck, C. S. (2003). Clarifying achievement goals and their impact. Journal of Personality and Social Psychology, 85(3), 541-553.

Grunig, J. E. (2013). Furnishing the Edifice: Ongoing Research on Public Relations as a Strategic Management Function. Journal of Public Relations Research, 18(2), 151–176.

Hartzband, P., & Groopman, J. (2018). Medical Taylorism. New England Journal of Medicine, 374(2), 106–108.

Hill, E. J., Hawkins, A. J., & Miller, B. C. (1996). Work and family in the virtual office: Perceived influences of mobile telework. *Family Relations, 45*(3), 293–301.

Hattie, J. (2009). Visible learning: A synthesis of over 800 meta-analyses relating to achievement. Routledge.

Hitt, M. A., Ireland, R. D., & Hoskisson, R. E. (2020). Strategic Management: Concepts and Cases: Competitiveness and Globalization. Cengage Learning.

Huang, Y. H., Li, Y., & Li, X. (2020). How toxic employees influence team performance: The roles of team collaboration and team conflict. Journal of Applied Social Psychology, 50(8), 486-498. https://doi.org/10.1111/j1/jasp.12654

Hunt, V., Layton, D., & Prince, S. (2015). Diversity matters. McKinsey & Company.

Johnston, M. (2012). Transformational School Leadership in Action: A Case Study of an Urban Elementary School. *Journal of Education and Learning, Vol 1, No 2 (2012)*. Retrieved from: https://files.eric.ed.gov/fulltext/EJ1083681.pdf

Judge, T. A., Thoresen, C. J., Bono, J. E., & Patton, G. K. (2001). The job satisfaction–job performance relationship: A qualitative and quantitative review. Psychological Bulletin, 127(3), 376.

Karl, K., Peluchette, J., & Hall, L. (2008). Give them something to smile about: a marketing strategy for recruiting and retaining volunteers. Journal of Nonprofit & Public Sector Marketing, 20(1), 71-96.

Kaufman, A. (2015). How the Golden State Warriors built a dominant culture from scratch. Forbes. Retrieved from https://www.forbes.com/sites/alanaglass/2015/06/17/how-the-golden-state-warriors-built-a-dominant-culture-from-scratch/?sh=2bc3df6b3c6f

Keller, J. (2020). Development and validation of the Keller influence indicator. *Journal of Leadership & Organizational Studies*, 27(1), 45–59. doi:10.1177/1548051818818045

Keller, K. L. (2013). Strategic brand management: Building, measuring, and managing brand equity. Pearson Education.

Keller, K. L., & Lehmann, D. R. (2006). Brands and branding: Research findings and future priorities. Marketing science, 25(6), 740-759.

Kent, M. L., & Taylor, M. (2002). Toward a dialogic theory of public relations. *Public relations review*, *28*(1), 21–37.

Kietzmann, J. H., Hermkens, K., McCarthy, I. P., & Silvestre, B. S. (2011). Social media? Get serious! Understanding the functional building blocks of social media. *Business Horizons*, *54*(3), 241–251.

Klein, C., Diaz-Granados, D., Salas, E., Le, H., Burke, C. S., Lyons, R., & Goodwin, G. F. (2009). Does team building work? *Small Group Research*, *40*(2), 181–222.

Koch, R. (1999). The 80/20 principle: The secret to achieving more with less. Doubleday.

Koch, R. (2011). *The 80/20 Principle: The Secret to Achieving More with Less*. Nicholas Brealey Publishing.

Kotter, J. P. (1996). Leading change. Harvard Business School Press

Kotter, J. P. (2012). Leading change. Harvard Business Press.

Laker, D. R., & Powell, J. L. (2011). The differences between hard and soft skills and their relative importance in the workplace. March 2011 Human Resource Development Quarterly 22(1):111 – 122

Lashinsky, A. (2018). How Microsoft CEO Satya Nadella rebuilt the company culture. Fortune. Retrieved from https://fortune.com/2018/07/19/microsoft-ceo-satya-nadella-company-culture/

Levasseur, R. E. (2013). People skills: Ensuring project success - A change management perspective. Interfaces, 41(2), 158-162.

Linnenluecke, M. K. (2017). Resilience in business and management research: A review of influential publications and a research agenda. International Journal of Management Reviews, 19(1), 4–30.

Lipman, V. (2016). The disturbing link between a leader's behavior and corporate culture. Forbes. Retrieved from https://www.forbes.com/sites/victorlipman/2016/02/21/the-disturbing-link-between-a-leaders-behavior-and-corporate-culture/

Locke, E. A., & Latham, G. P. (2019). Building a practically useful theory of goal setting and task motivation: A 35-year odyssey. *American Psychologist*, 74(2), 182–195. doi:10.1037/amp0000400

London, M., & Smither, J. W. (2021). Performance management. In S. Zedeck (Ed.), *APA Handbook of Industrial and Organizational Psychology, Vol. 2: Selecting and Developing Members for the organization* (pp. 195–235). American Psychological Association.

Luo, X., & Bhattacharya, C. B. (2009). The debate over doing good: Corporate social performance, strategic marketing levers, and firm-idiosyncratic risk. *Journal of marketing*, 73(6), 198–213.

Marques, J., & Lee, M. (2011). The global diamond industry: Economics and development (Vol. 2).

Maurer, T. J., Weiss, E. M., & Barbeite, F. G. (2003). A model of involvement in work-related learning and development activity: The effects of individual, situational, motivational, and age variables. Journal of Applied Psychology, 88(4), 707-724.

McDowell, T. (2004). Fun at work: Scale development, confirmatory factor analysis, and links to organizational outcomes.

(Order No. 3145202, The University of North Carolina at Charlotte). ProQuest Dissertations and Theses.

McNall, L. A., Nicklin, J. M., & Masuda, A. D. (2010). A meta-analytic review of the consequences associated with work–family enrichment. *Journal of Business and Psychology, 25*(3), 381–396.

Medina, M. (2018). How Steve Kerr's coaching style has made the Warriors a powerhouse. Mercury News. Retrieved from https://www.mercurynews.com/2018/05/29/how-steve-kerrs-coaching-style-has-made-the-warriors-a-powerhouse/

Meadows, D. H. (1999). Leverage Points: Places to Intervene in a System. Sustainability Institute.

Men, L. R. (2014). Strategic internal communication: Transformational leadership, communication channels, and employee satisfaction. Management Communication Quarterly, 28(2), 264–284.

Musk, E. (2017). Elon Musk's Master Plan (Part Deux). Tesla, Inc.

Nadella, S. (2017). Hit Refresh: The Quest to Rediscover Microsoft's Soul and Imagine a Better Future for Everyone. Harper Business.

Nisen, M. (2013). Satya Nadella's Transformation Of Working Culture From The Man Who Wrote The Book On It. Quartz. Retrieved from: https://qz.com/176354/satya-nadellas-transformation-of-microsofts-work-culture-from-the-man-who-literally-wrote-the-book-on-it/

O'Leary, M. B., Mortensen, M., & Woolley, A. W. (2011). Multiple team membership: A theoretical model of its effects on productivity and learning for individuals and teams. *Academy of Management Review, 36*(3), 461–478.

Oswald, A. J., Proto, E., & Sgroi, D. (2015). Happiness and productivity. *Journal of Labor Economics, 33*(4), 789–822.

Ovide, S. (2018). How Microsoft's comeback led to a $100 billion sales year. Bloomberg. Retrieved from https://www.bloomberg.com/opinion/articles/2018-07-19/microsoft-s-comeback-recipe-a-100-billion-sales-year

Pajo, K., Coetzer, A., & Guenole, N. (2010). Formal development opportunities and withdrawal behaviors by employees in small and medium-sized enterprises. Journal of Small Business Management, 48(3), 281-301.

Palgrave Macmillan. Patagonia. (2020). Our Reason For Being. Retrieved from Patagonia website: https://www.patagonia.com/home/

Pearson, C. M., & Porath, C. L. (2005). On the nature, consequences, and remedies of workplace incivility: No time for "nice"? Think again. Academy of Management Perspectives, 19(1), 7–18.

Porath, C., & Pearson, C. (2013). The price of incivility. Harvard Business Review, 91(1-2), pp. 114–121.

Ravitch, D. (2016). Reign of error: The hoax of the privatization movement and the danger to America's public schools. Vintage.

Rawlins, B. (2008). Give the emperor a mirror: Toward developing a stakeholder measurement of organizational transparency. *Journal of public relations research, 21*(1), 71–99.

Rogelberg, S. G., Scott, C. W., & Kello, J. E. (2007). The science and fiction of meetings. MIT Sloan Management Review, 48(2), 18.
Smith, A. (1776). The Wealth of Nations. London: W. Strahan and T. Cadell.

Rynes, S. L., Bartunek, J. M., Dutton, J. E., & Margolis, J. D. (2012). Care and compassion through an organizational lens:

Opening up new possibilities. *Academy of Management Review*, *37*(4), 503–523.

Serge, P. (2022). Talent management: A strategic approach for the modern organization. McGraw-Hill Education.

Senge, P. M. (2006). The fifth discipline: The art and practice of the learning organization. Currency.

Senge, P. M. (1990). The fifth discipline: The art and practice of the learning organization. Doubleday/Currency.
Skarzauskiene, A. (2010). Managing complexity: systems thinking as a catalyst of the organization performance. Measuring Business Excellence, 14(4), 49-64.

Skiba, R. J., Horner, R. H., Chung, C. G., Rausch, M. K., May, S. L., & Tobin, T. (2011). Race is not neutral: A national investigation of African American and Latino disproportionality in school discipline. School Psychology Review, 40(1), 85-107.

Solomon, C. M. (1992). The corporate culture survival guide: Sense and nonsense about culture change. *Personnel*, *69*(10), 77.

Slavin, R. E. (1996). Education for all. Lisse: Swets & Zeitlinger.

Starbucks. (2020). Global Social Impact Report 2020. Retrieved from Starbucks website: https://www.starbucks.com/responsibility/global-report

Steinberg, L. (2001). We know some things: Parent–adolescent relationships in retrospect and prospect. Journal of Research on Adolescence, 11(1), 1-19.

Sterman, J. D. (2000). Business dynamics: systems thinking and modeling for a complex world. Irwin/McGraw-Hill.

Stewart, G. L., & Barrick, M. R. (2000). Team structure and performance: Assessing the mediating role of intrateam process and the moderating role of task type. Academy of Management Journal, 43(2), 135–148.

Sutton, R. I. (2007). The no asshole rule: Building a civilized workplace and surviving one that isn't. Business Plus

Sweller, J. (1988). Cognitive load during problem solving: Effects on learning. Cognitive Science, 12(2), 257–285.

Tews, M. J., Michel, J. W., & Allen, D. G. (2014). Fun and friends: The impact of workplace fun and constituent attachment on turnover in a hospitality context. Human Relations, 67(8), 923-946.

Tews, M. J., Michel, J. W., & Bartlett, A. (2012). The fundamental role of workplace fun in applicant attraction. *Journal of Leadership & Organizational Studies, 19*(1), 105–114.

Tews, M. J., Michel, J. W., & Noe, R. A. (2017). Does fun promote learning? The relationship between fun in the workplace and informal learning. Journal of Vocational Behavior, 98, 46-55.

Thompson, L. (2008). *Making the team: A guide for managers* (3rd ed.). Pearson Prentice Hall.

Tulgan, B. (2016). The Great Generational Shift: The Emerging Post-Boomer Workforce. Rainmaker Thinking, Inc.

Universum. (2020). World's Most Attractive Employers 2020. Universum Global. Retrieved from: https://universumglobal.com/wmae-2020/

Vance, A. (2015). Elon Musk: Tesla, SpaceX, and the Quest for a Fantastic Future. HarperCollins.

Vischer, J. C. (2007). The effects of the physical environment on job performance: towards a theoretical model of workspace stress.

Stress and Health: Journal of the International Society for the Investigation of Stress, 23(3), 175-184

Watson, T., & Noble, P. (2007). *Evaluating public relations: A best practice guide to public relations planning, research & evaluation.* Kogan Page Publishers.

Whitaker, T. (2021). What great teachers do differently: 17 things that matter most. Routledge.

Whitaker, T., Whitaker, B., & Lumpa, D. (2013). Managing difficult people: Turning 'negatives' into 'positives'. Larchmont, NY: Eye on Education.

Whitaker, T. (2012). *Shifting the Monkey: The Art of protecting good people from Liars, criers, and other slackers.* Solution Tree Press.

Whitaker, T. (2012). What great principals do differently: Eighteen things that matter most (2nd ed.). Eye on Education.

Whitaker, T. (2002). Dealing with difficult teachers (2nd ed.). Eye on Education.

Wuchty, S., Jones, B. F., & Uzzi, B. (2007). The Increasing Dominance of Teams in the Production of Knowledge. Science, 316(5827), 1036-1039.

DR. LEANNE SALAZAR-MONTOYA'S BIO

Dr. LeAnne Salazar-Montoya, Assistant Professor at the University of Las Vegas Professional Biography for LeAnne Salazar-Montoya, Ph.D.

Dr. LeAnne Salazar-Montoya is a lifelong educator and public servant originally from Northern New Mexico, where she has dedicated twenty years of leadership, research, and service to the causes of education, social equity, and the leveling of the playing field for the next generation of students, teachers, and leaders. As a first-generation college graduate from her family, she holds an associate's, a bachelor's, two master's, and a doctoral degree in the field of education. Like so many women, Dr. Montoya also holds an honorary degree in Motherhood as a proud mother of three. Her research in educational leadership, inclusivity, and Latina superintendency has been presented at state and national conferences and published in academic forums such as the Journal for Research in Education. Alongside her research interests, she remains actively involved with professional organizations such as ALAS (Association of Latino Administrators and Superintendents), where she serves the board as the national chair for Professional Learning

Growth and Development and the Vice President of the Nevada Chapter of ALAS.

In my journey as a social justice and equity educator and advocate, I am deeply committed to cultivating the next generation of school leaders who share my passion and values. I recognize that lasting change can only be achieved by nurturing a new wave of leaders who are well-versed in the principles of justice and equity and committed to integrating them into the very fabric of our educational systems. By imparting the importance of empathy, inclusivity, and critical thinking, I aim to empower these future leaders to champion social justice in the classroom and beyond. Together, we can build a network of change agents who will not only move the needle but ultimately transform the landscape of our educational institutions and society, ushering in an era where opportunity and fairness are accessible to all, regardless of their background or circumstances.

The significance of making a lasting impact is paramount in my professional ethos. Titles and accolades may shine momentarily, but their luster fades if not accompanied by a profound and enduring influence on others. For me, professional fulfillment lies in the ripple effect of my efforts, in the lives I touch, and the positive transformations I catalyze. It is not merely about reaching the summit of a career trajectory; instead, it is about carving a path that future leaders can traverse more easily and with greater success. To me, the essence of leadership is found in the positive difference we make in the lives of those we serve. Witnessing the growth, empowerment, and gratitude of others is the true measure of a leader's impact. Through their appreciation, leadership's real success is gauged, knowing that the seeds planted have germinated into a garden of sustainable change. In essence, leadership is not about the leader but about the enduring legacy of progress and empowerment that one leaves behind, shaping the landscape for generations to come.

Her expertise and rise to leadership positions are the result of a trailblazing woman who has worn many hats over the years as a mother, a teacher, an administrator, an HR director, a small business owner, a school superintendent, and most recently as an assistant professor at the University of Las Vegas where she is channeling her educational philosophy and decades-long career into tomorrow's leaders. In this rewarding role, Dr. Montoya invests her time in preparing her students for leadership positions in their communities.

DR. CHRISTOPHER BONN'S BIO

Dr. Christopher Bonn is a dynamic and accomplished Superintendent with a track record of success in administration and public education leadership. With over 18 years of experience, including nine years as a Superintendent in Arizona, California, and New Mexico, he has demonstrated his versatility and unconventional leadership style that gets immediate results.

Dr. Bonn has participated in reorganizing several districts with significant improvements in performance and achievement despite limited and declining resources and revenue. His expertise in reorganization, problem-solving, and providing solutions has proved to be a tremendous asset to the organizations in which he has worked.

As a strategic and operational authority, Dr. Bonn is well-versed in developing and implementing an organization's vision. He has facilitated intergovernmental agreements, networking with other businesses and corporations, created and revised policies and guidelines, and is familiar with credentialing and certification processes. Dr. Bonn is proficient in international teachers' exchange and Visa Processes and experienced in tribal and indigenous affairs while working to diversify systems in the organization and make practices more equitable.

Dr. Bonn's motivational and inspiring leadership style focuses on teamwork, equity, and diversifying organizational opportunities. He has extensive experience in staff development, coaching, budget management, and moving organizations forward with limited staff and resources.

Dr. Bonn holds a Doctor of Education in Leadership, a Master of Education in Leadership, and a B.A. in Counseling Psychology/Special Education.

He has worked in various positions, including Superintendent of Schools, Interim Director of Special Education, Principal, Assistant Principal, Teacher, Varsity Football and Wrestling Coach, and Consultant. As a mentor to talented leaders, he has successfully guided and built leadership capability, resulting in 100% of individuals mentored being promoted to executive-level positions within the organization.

Dr. Bonn is a proud native of Tucson, Arizona, with a Latino heritage and a love for the outdoors. He enjoys archery, fly fishing, dancing, hiking, and travel. Dr. Bonn is also trained in culinary arts and loves to cook. He comes from a family that owns a ranch in Tucson, where he enjoys working with all the livestock and animals and riding horses. In 2023, he will become the first-time grandfather to his son Andrew's child.

Dr. Bonn's unique leadership style, versatile expertise, and passion for life make him a compelling leader.

CONNECT WITH
Dr. Christopher Bonn

For bulk purchases, speaking engagements, comments, and questions, reach out to Dr. Christopher Bonn at:

Chris@BonFireLeadershipSolutions.com

www.bonfireleadershipsolutions.com

Published by C.D. Johnson

www.diverseskillscenter.com
support@diverseskillscenter.com

www.ingramcontent.com/pod-product-compliance
Lightning Source LLC
Chambersburg PA
CBHW070403240426
43661CB00056B/2518